Value Stream Mapping for Healthcare Made Easy

Endorsements for Value Stream Mapping for Healthcare Made Easy by Cindy Jimmerson

"Following her publication A3 Problem Solving for Healthcare, Cindy Jimmerson has produced another excellent book that demonstrates why Value Stream Maps are a fundamental component in applying Lean TPS and how using the A3 and VSM enables you to see the bigger picture and zero in on a specific problem. The selection of case studies reflects the range of common problems across the whole healthcare system. A must read for all."

Lesley Wright
Director – Diagnostics
NHS Improvement

"This book is an invaluable resource for all involved in implementation of Lean in Healthcare. Every reader from novice to veteran practitioner will find what they are looking for here. Cindy Jimmerson has put it all together in a practical guide that covers big concepts, all the technical details, and illustrated case studies that clarify how all of the tools and concepts work together. Jimmerson has demystified the Value Stream Map and made it an actionable tool for all!"

Mimi Falbo
Mimi Falbo LLC

"Throughout my nearly 20 year career at Toyota and my consulting work beyond, I have coached many clients on Lean Thinking in a wide range of industries both public and private. Along the way, I have seen many 'translations' of Toyota's approach to other industries and business applications. Sadly, most miss the mark. Some by a lot!

I am pleased however that Cindy Jimmerson's work here is not only true to it's lean 'roots' in Toyota but she has added to the overall body of knowledge in significant ways that make logical extensions and rational adaptations to fit her clients' unique needs.

I would highly recommend this book to anyone desiring to genuinely adopt the Toyota approach to the healthcare industry and to do so with confidence. This is the real deal."

Ken Pilone
President
Sterling Methods Consulting Group, LLC

"This is an outstanding book, the best one available on Value Stream Mapping. Cindy Jimmerson is a remarkable teacher and a pioneer in lean thinking. Her visual organization in this book (and her book on A3 problem solving) make VSM immediately accessible and useful. The case studies are superb. As a practicing Anesthesiologist, Hospice Physician, and Medical Director, I was fortunate to recently take her course, and I will be applying the information in this book to healthcare for the rest of my career."

Shaun Sullivan, MD
Partner, Bellingham Anesthesia Associates
Anesthesia Medical Director, Skagit Valley Hospital
Whatcom Hospice Medical Director

"Value stream mapping for healthcare is indeed 'made easy'. Cindy has found the ideal balance of information and application. The examples, step-by-step instructions and 'simple, yet elegant' flow of information is ideal for anyone interested in developing their lean knowledge. Well worth reading, and applying."

Barb Bouche
Director, CPI
Seattle Children's Hospital

"As a former student of Cindy's and owner of many health care processes I can tell you that this book is a remarkable journey from the complex to the simple. By using the tools taught and the elegant examples in this book, one can learn to see apparently complex problems broken down into manageable processes through the use of Cindy's practical application of value stream mapping. When I have used her techniques, once the process was really mapped to reflect the true state of affairs, solutions jump off the page. Unlike other dry management dissertations, this book is rich with real health care examples drawn from the author's own clinical and managerial experience. Cindy is a remarkable teacher and this book captures the essence of her teaching on the effective use of value stream mapping in health care."

John Salyer RRT-NPS, MBA, FAARC
Author of Managing the Respiratory Care Department
Director Respiratory Therapy Services
Seattle Children's Hospital and Research Institute

"Cindy Jimmerson is a proven and well-known practicioner of lean methods in healthcare. Her book is full of varied case studies that beautifully illustrate the power of the Value Stream Mapping method and how it fits into a lean transformation journey."

Mark Graban
Author of Lean Hospitals: Improving Quality, Patient Safety, and Employee Satisfaction
Founder of www.leanblog.org

Value Stream Mapping for Healthcare Made Easy

Cindy Jimmerson

Illustrated by Amy Jimmerson and Herman Ranpurnia

CRC Press
Taylor & Francis Group
Boca Raton · London · New York

CRC Press is an imprint of the
Taylor & Francis Group, an **informa** business
A PRODUCTIVITY PRESS BOOK

Productivity Press
Taylor & Francis Group
270 Madison Avenue
New York, NY 10016

International Standard Book Number-13: 978-1-4200-7852-7 (Softcover)

Library of Congress Cataloging-in-Publication Data

Jimmerson, Cindy LeDuc.
    Value stream mapping for healthcare made easy / Cindy Jimmerson.
       p. ; cm.
    Includes bibliographical references and index.
    ISBN 978-1-4200-7852-7 (hardcover : alk. paper)
    1. Health services administration. 2. Value analysis (Cost control) 3. Organizational effectiveness. 4. Just-in-time systems. I. Title.
    [DNLM: 1. Delivery of Health Care--organization & administration. 2. Efficiency, Organizational. 3. Health Care Reform--methods. W 84.1 J61v 2010]

RA971.J48 2010
362.1--dc22
                                                         2009004796

Visit the Taylor & Francis Web site at
http://www.taylorandfrancis.com

and the Productivity Press Web site at
http://www.productivitypress.com

As always, for Amy and Julia.

Contents

Acknowledgments

The basic work for this book was developed through study and practice by the author, mentoring by manufacturers, healthcare workers, and educators from around the world, and the generous support of the National Science Foundation, grant 0115352 (2001–2004). More importantly, with gratitude the author thanks the staffs and leaders of more than 60 healthcare organizations who have used this simple but powerful method of looking at work differently as their first step toward improving healthcare delivery. It is their feedback and suggestions that have contributed to the diverse applications of value stream mapping (VSM) for healthcare. The following individuals have added specific simplicity and elegance to make VSM a straightforward practice even for the beginning student of lean thinking:

- Vicki Baum
- Amy Jimmerson
- Susan Sheehy
- Durward Sobek
- Jayne Ottman
- Dorothy Weber

While some of the VSMs in Part II have been slightly altered to make a teaching point, each one of the examples is taken from real work done by real people in the course of recognizing problems and improving the delivery of care. In particular, the following organizations have contributed experience and enthusiasm to the case studies in Part II of this book. The author acknowledges them with deep gratitude:

- Community Medical Center, Missoula, Montana
- Northern Arizona Health, Flagstaff, Arizona
- Centennial Medical Center, Nashville, Tennessee
- St. Vincent Hospital, Billings, Montana
- St. Patrick Hospital and Health Center, Missoula, Montana

A very special thanks to Dilesh Patel (GumshoeKI, Inc.) for his detailed contributions to this text. The mastery of simple Value Stream Mapping inevitably leads to the creative addition of more valuable information and the need to share the work well done. Dilesh's contributions will undoubtedly launch the expansion of simple mapping skills.

Introduction

My experience with value stream mapping (VSM) for healthcare resulted from a very fortunate opportunity provided by the National Science Foundation in 2000. Through a grant awarded to Montana State University (MSU) (NSF grant 0115352, Applying the principles of the Toyota Production System to healthcare, 2000–2002), coinvestigated by myself and Dr. Durward Sobek, a professor at the engineering school at MSU, I was funded for 3 years to explore the possibility of using concepts and practices of the Toyota Production System (TPS) in a healthcare setting. It was a goal from the outset to apply these principles and methods in every department of the host healthcare organization. To attempt to do this, the application needed to be easy to learn, easy to teach, and relevant to all kinds of work. These requirements, coupled with Dr. Sobek's studies and personal experience at Toyota, led our exploration to the then-emerging work of Steven Spear.

At the conclusion of research for his doctoral work in 1999, Harvard PhD candidate Steven Spear, with Harvard Business School professor Kent Bowen, described the concepts of "ideal" and the "four rules in use." [The concept of ideal is originally credited to Dr. Russell L. Ackoff in T. Lee and T. Woll, "Reflections on the Idealized Design Planning Process," *CQM Journal* 11, no. 2 (2003).] In their landmark paper, "Decoding the DNA of the Toyota Production System" [S. Spear and H. Kent Bowen, *Harvard Business Review*, September–October (1999), pp. 97–106], they concluded that these simple concepts and rules were the fundamental drivers of the Toyota culture of work. While simple in concept, the consistent practice of ideal and the four rules is applicable to any business model, especially healthcare.

Toyota's Role in Lean

When discussing continuous improvement it is impossible to overlook the contribution of the Toyota Motor Company. Their work has led to the development of this book and scores of others about Lean and process improvement. Toyota generously shares their knowledge with the world, and the world listens. Why?

Although they lagged behind U.S. manufacturers in production after World War II, they have grown to be not only the largest auto manufacturer in the world, but also, for 58 years, the most profitable. This has led many to study what is now called the Toyota Production System (TPS) to learn how they achieved their current market position.

The Toyota we know today started as a department within the Toyoda Automatic Loom Works, Ltd. According to Toyota, the root of the TPS began with Sakichi Toyoda, who constantly focused on the elimination of all waste to efficiently produce automatic looms. While in the loom business, Kiichiro Toyoda, son of Sakichi Toyoda, visited the United States and Europe to learn about the manufacture of automobiles, and when orders for looms slowed in the 1930s, the family decided to move into the automotive industry. In 1937, the Toyota Motor Company, Ltd., was formally established.

It was not until the early 1950s that Eiji Toyoda and Taiichi Ohno, Toyota's chief production engineer, began experimenting with systems that would ultimately support their strategy to become a full-range auto manufacturer. They had many challenges, not the least of which was the lack of capital resources to invest in a mass production system. As a result of their work, the TPS was born. Their early logo from the 1950s, "Good thinking, good products," is one that continues to live through expanded adaptations in many industries in the world today.

Around that same time, the Japanese met an American by the name of W. Edwards Deming. He believed that if Japanese manufacturers would build the best quality products, customers would buy them. Quality had to be built into every step of the production process, and he promoted the training and development of workers to accomplish that task. His teaching was in stark contrast to the mass producers of the time who inspected quality at the end of the production line and experienced costly rework. These other manufacturers also expected workers to focus only on specific, repetitive tasks without the opportunity to improve their work, which led to poor working conditions and a frustrated workforce.

The leaders of Toyota took Dr. Deming very seriously and focused on building the highest quality vehicles on the market. In Japan today, the highest award for manufacturing excellence is still the Deming Award. Toyota has created a culture where everyone is challenged to eliminate waste and defects; they support all employees in improving work processes. The TPS has helped Toyota become the world leader in auto manufacturing. Their success is worth following, as their culture of striving toward perfect quality and relentlessly eliminating waste is applicable to any industry.

Toyota enjoys some claims to fame that would be enviable in any organization. Their record for employee satisfaction and low turnover is exemplary and not an accident. Toyota reveres its employees, considering each of them a scientist who is skilled in problem solving and discovery. Every employee is expected to *think*. This expectation is fundamental in their structure as a learning organization. Each worker uses A3 thinking in his or her daily work, and the concepts behind this problem-solving method are those that build confidence at the front line and in the boardroom. Toyota recognizes its workers as its greatest asset and has the best history of avoiding layoffs in the automotive industry. Development of individual talent and thinking is the backbone of Toyota's quality and fiscal success.

In October 2004, I was fortunate to hear Art Niimi, CEO of Toyota America, speak at the national conference of the Association for Manufacturing Excellence in Cincinnati, Ohio. Speaking to a packed room of 1200 attendees, Mr. Niimi's single slide, which illuminated the back wall of the triple ballroom in which the lunchtime presentation was made, read simply, "THINK DEEPLY." The title of his talk was "Respect for Man and Respect for Mankind." There was no mention in the title, slides, or content of cutting costs, creaming the competition, laying off staff, or taking over the world of auto manufacturing. Instead, his dignified presence and elegant manner spoke only to respecting the people doing the work and respect for mankind and the earth on which we rely. His message was powerful and crystal clear: Think deeply. At the end of the very moving presentation, Mr. Niimi responded to several questions from the audience, one of which made me want to jump on the table and cheer! He was asked why, with the success that puts Toyota in the global media spotlight almost daily, did not he or someone from Toyota write a book telling people how to do what Toyota has done. There was a palpable pause and silence as everyone in the room awaited his answer, which was, "If I did, it would only be two pages." The response of those new to lean was quizzical; they did not get it. Those of us who have lived the practices completely understood the message. To make it complicated is to lose the essence of thinking deeply.

This message creates a dilemma for those of us who have lived and grown up in the world of traditional command-and-control management. We were not encouraged to think deeply, but rather to report problems up the ladder so someone else could come up with a fix. It has been the unrealistic (and unfair!) expectation that management and the senior leadership team should create fixes for problems in work from which they are far removed. It has been the expectation that frontline workers must make those changes happen, despite their eye-rolling acknowledgement that the fix will likely fail. We have failed not only our workers but our organizations by *not* expecting deep thinking to be practiced daily by every worker. We have lost the knowledge locked in our collective intelligence.

Convincing well respected and accomplished workers to think deeply, which usually requires thinking ***differently***, be they invested professionals or temps from a labor pool, is not easy. But as Toyota and so many of its emulators have proven, when bright, motivated workers are given clear direction and objective information, with fair guidance and encouragement in a safe environment, they support change that they create. The elegance of a method like value stream mapping that can initiate and excite the willingness to change can be appreciated only when it is seen in action.

Advantages of VSM

Value stream mapping, a component of lean thinking, has a number of advantages, all of which apply to the healthcare industry:

- **Value stream maps (as well as A3 problem-solving reports—see Chapter 6) are done on the front side only of an 11 inch × 17 inch sheet of paper.** A limited area for problem analysis forces the problem solver to choose issues that are specific enough to complete on one sheet. This ensures that the work is of a scope that can be realistically completed, quickly demonstrating successful change and motivating workers to do even more problem solving.
- **Lean thinking occurs in the course of work.** Large numbers of staff do not have to be gathered for extended times to do value stream mapping and A3 problem solving. Coaches can be recognized and easily trained to help staff validate observations and participate in lean thinking without leaving their work sites.
- **Lean thinking is intuitive and easy to learn and remember.** Healthcare workers did not enter the profession to become management engineers or spend all their time improving processes; they came to this work to take care of people. Lean thinking is logical thinking based on the familiar scientific method of problem solving that is easy to learn and teach and requires no technical proficiency.
- **Lean thinking is satisfying to everyone who uses it, particularly frontline workers.** Lean thinking is an easy-to-learn and easy-to-teach method that staff can use to remove the frustrations of their daily work that are created by weak and unsupportive processes. This ability to be involved with creating a better way to work has been exceptionally well received by frontline workers, those Toyota recognizes as resident experts. Lean thinking involves frontline workers in improving work that is meaningful to them, at a level at which they can see and appreciate the changes they have participated in creating. In this era of current and impending healthcare worker shortages, this satisfaction is essential to retaining good workers.
- **Lean thinking develops stronger leaders.** As a method for deeply understanding the work for which they are ultimately responsible and for facilitating change and improvement in the organizations, VSMs and A3s are clear and objective communication tools that include the knowledge of all levels of workers in the value stream. Along with worker engagement comes confidence of the frontline in leadership's commitment to improvement.
- **Lean thinking can be used to create better and fewer meetings.** Conducting a lean meeting using value stream maps and the A3 problem-solving process can greatly reduce the time and number of meetings required to achieve the work of the agenda.

■ **Value stream maps and A3 reports are both a template for problem solving and documentation of the effort.** When value stream maps and A3 documents are stored in a three-ring binder, governing board members, physicians, senior leaders, as well as staff from other departments can review them. This allows cross-departmental sharing of process changes and generates even more problem-solving ideas. Software has been developed to easily convert pencil-drawn value stream maps and A3s for sharing, presenting, and archiving (see Chapter 7).

■ **Value Stream Mapping is the springboard of process innovation.** Once any process is deeply understood to the detail that value stream mapping creates, limitless innovations in the ability to offer the requested service arise. This can be used in building new facilities and IT that better support the work and in everyday improvement of safety, patient and worker satisfaction, and affordability.

What You Will Find In This Book

This is a two-part book that includes the following material:

Part I: The Basics of Value Stream Mapping

This part introduces you—whether you are a lean novice or an experienced lean practitioner—to an easy-to-learn, easy-to-teach method for lean healthcare. You discover how to see all the value-added and non-value-added activities in the delivery of a requested service or product. By looking at work this way, the staff doing the work as well as the designers and executors of organizational strategies of that work will be able to evaluate, create, and communicate innovation in your workplace.

Value stream mapping, based on rock-solid concepts proven by the Toyota Production System, is represented here as the fundamental structure of lean thinking. I refer to many features and methods of lean thinking that contribute to improving work, but VSM is the first look at a process that gets to the point and provides a deep understanding of how the work happens now and where the work is not reliable and consistent. This information acts as a springboard for improving the process; I also discuss the future state map as a progressive document for capturing and illustrating the anticipated better way to work.

A3 problem solving, the other concept tool of lean thinking, is briefly discussed in this book as well to demonstrate the evolution of thinking from the system picture of the value stream map to the specific change of activities refined with an A3. Fuller texts specifically written on A3 problem solving offer more detail for the curious.

Part II: Case Studies

In this part we will review real value stream maps completed at real healthcare facilities. These maps have been produced by teams of healthcare administrators, managers, physicians, and staff members from every department of various healthcare organizations. Most participants were not experienced with lean thinking, and for many these were their first engagements with lean methods. The sources of individual value stream maps are not identified, but grateful recognition of the contributors is made on the Acknowledgments page in the front of the book.

In the review of each of the maps we will consider some or all of the following, with consideration for learning value:

■ How and by whom the mapped process was selected for improvement
■ The composite of the improvement team engaged in the mapping exercises
■ The method used for data collection
■ The initial current state map
■ The future state map
■ Specific problems identified that developed into A3s for problem solving or other lean tools used
■ The plan for accomplishing the improvements
■ Outcomes of the improvement work
■ Unique discoveries made during this work

THE BASICS OF VALUE STREAM MAPPING

Chapter 1

Identifying Waste in Healthcare

Taiichi Ohno, the man credited with the development of the Toyota Production System (TPS) in the early 1950s, identified the seven *mudas* (sources of waste) in manufacturing, which include the following:

■ Conveyance
■ Motion
■ Waiting
■ Overprocessing
■ Inventory
■ Defects
■ Overproduction

While there are likely many more sources of *muda* that are unique to every industry, in this chapter I have adapted Ohno's list, with only minor modification to the first *muda*, to make it more pertinent to healthcare. The term seven *mudas* is well recognized by advocates of TPS, but in a slightly converted list for this industry, I have combined "conveyance" and "motion" (my apologies to Toyota purists!) and included "confusion." This was not an arbitrary decision, but one based on thousands of hours of direct observation in which highly skilled and educated caregivers spent many hours of their day asking questions like "Where does this go?", "What do I do with this (thing/person/information)?", "I can't read this writing, what does this say?", "What happens next?", and so on. Since 2000 I have received many suggestions for adding to the list of sources of waste—all good ones! But I had to stop somewhere. So I encourage you not to be stuck on these seven wastes as an exact prescription, but to recognize that there are basic systemic failures that occur regularly in every industry, and identifying the ones specific to our own work is incredibly valuable. It is amazing how easy it is to see elements of waste in daily work once you review and understand them. Here is my rendition of the seven *mudas* for healthcare:

- Confusion
- Motion/conveyance
- Waiting
- Overprocessing
- Inventory
- Defects
- Overproduction

Waste 1: Confusion

Patient safety is now and always has been at the forefront of every caregiver's mind. The medical errors that have been reported in recent academic and media exposés have alarmed and infuriated the general population and devastated the morale of healthcare workers. Failure of processes to support healthcare workers in doing their good work is very often rooted in confusion.

A casual observer in a hospital anywhere in the world would likely be alarmed if they focused only on the questions of clarification that are asked every day. In one study conducted by Anita Tucker and Steven Spear (2006), nurses on a busy medical unit experienced 8.4 work system failures per shift. Working with scores of hospitals of all sizes and levels of sophistication in the past 9 years, my colleagues and I have recorded very similar results, with nurses spending as much as 65% of their time looking for things they could not find, clarifying information and instructions that were unclear, and doing redundant paperwork (Jimmerson et al. 2005). Confusion included questions like the following:

- "What do I do with this requisition?"
- "What does this order mean?"
- "Does anyone know what I'm supposed to do with this?"
- "Where do we store the...?"
- "Where are the reports for...?"

Similar questions are asked thousands of times in the daily course of caring for patients.

Although resolution of the confusion was necessary for caregivers to get their jobs done or meet regulatory requirements, most of their activities did not add value to the patient. And to no one's surprise, these confusion-laden activities were recognized by the hardworking and motivated staff as being a waste of their time and a source of great frustration.

Imagine if the work process were so intuitive that answers were built into the process and the current time spent and frustration experienced could be eliminated. In reducing the confusion *muda* alone lies the potential to capture a great deal of worker capacity, decrease worker frustration, and reduce the opportunity for errors in patient care.

Waste 2: Motion/Conveyance

Motion/conveyance refers to the physical movement required to get a simple task accomplished and to move people and products from place to place. Redundant reaching for items that are not handy and walking to another location only to return to the starting point to resume work are examples of motion by a worker that do not add value to the patient or customer. Conveyance of patients and materials from room to room or department to department is also wasted motion. Recall a recent patient experience of your own in your healthcare network: Was everything you needed located in the same department, same building, on the same block, or within the same campus?

When you start to observe and make note of motion, you will see these "loops" in action (see Figure 1.1). To visualize time-saving opportunity, imagine that the work could happen with continuous flow, in a straight line, without those loops.

Waste 3: Waiting

Delay in service is often the result of time spent doing nothing but waiting for something to occur. It may be waiting for a procedure to be done, a medication to arrive, or a physician order to be given. Imagine the waste created when the radiology staff is standing by waiting for a patient to arrive from the intensive care unit (ICU), the ICU and patient are standing by waiting for a transporter to arrive and take the patient to the radiology department, and the transporter is madly scrambling to find the right stretcher on which to transport the patient. And imagine the discomfort, anxiety, and maybe even doubt that the patient suffers as he or she watches the staff perform poorly.

While we are accustomed to considering delays annoying, the implications can be much greater when treatment is held up for the patient. Everyone who has sat in a waiting room anxiously waiting for a diagnosis for himself or a loved one understands the waste and distress created by delay. And think about the cost of the simple ICU scenario just described.

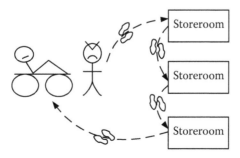

Figure 1.1

Waste 4: Overprocessing

Overprocessing refers to doing more activities than is necessary to complete a piece of work. Duplicating work that has been already been done in a different software system or in another department in a slightly different way is common in healthcare and is an opportunity to free up worker time. Think of how many times you enter a patient's demographic or personal history information during one hospital visit!

Buried in the steps that it takes to accomplish a task is a tremendous potential for improvement. When unnecessary hands (and brains!) touch the patient or product, waste is created that can be avoided with a smart redesign. The goal in fixing any process is to never reduce the safety or quality to the patient, but rather to enhance those strengths and remove the weak or redundant activities that do not add value.

Waste 5: Inventory

Perhaps one of the easiest sources of waste to physically measure and to assign a dollar value to is wasted inventory. This may be in stored supplies that are obsolete, duplicated, or unnecessary, or in missed charges for items used. Inefficient inventory control systems—ones that do not support the worker's demands—cause "supermarketing" or stockpiling of supplies not because they are needed, but *in case* they may be needed. Due to a lack of confidence in inventory processes that they have seen fail, workers may stash the items they need so that they know exactly where to find crucial supplies, if necessary. As an example, if a daily average of 30 abdominal pads are used on a busy surgical floor but the nurses have learned that sometimes they run out or sometimes they are needed in a room distant from the storeroom, they may gather more than is needed and put them at the patient's bedside or hide them in a personal locker or a convenient space closer to their assigned rooms. The restocker will see a dramatic depletion of pads and restock. Multiply stashing three abdominal pads times seven nurses and the actual inventory could nearly double, while the actual use (and charges) stays the same. Recognizing these patterns and involving the staff in redesigning the work can result in dramatic reductions in the cost of materials!

The other opportunity for engaging staff in materials waste reduction is a periodic review of worksite stores to identify obsolete or out-of-date inventory. The lean practice of 5S for updating stores and maintaining order is simple and easy to monitor. Here is what the five S's stand for:

■ Sort
■ Straighten
■ Sweep

- Standardize
- Sustain

There are many free references to the practice of 5S on the Internet, as well as a number of books that delve deeper into this topic.

With the objective of having the right item in the right place at the right time, it is easy to observe a healthcare worker in motion and see opportunities to put essential supplies at hand. This practice not only averts the previously mentioned inventory wastes, but as with most sources of *muda*, valuable worker time is also not wasted.

Another way to consider inventory as a source of waste is to look into the waiting room of a hospital and see the patients who are waiting as "inventory." You begin to see the bottleneck in flow that creates the delay in care as your "inventory" builds in the waiting room. Here, too, you want to have the right patient at the right place at the right time.

Waste 6: Defects

No one who can read a magazine or newspaper is unaware of the current focus on medical errors. Defects as a source of waste in healthcare are staggering when one considers the measures of dollars wasted, life years lost, litigation, worker turnover, and a general lack of confidence in healthcare as an industry. And no measure can be assigned to the agony of loss or suffering caused by medical errors.

Although some errors are deemed "operator errors," behind almost every one of those is a process failure. From getting the right name in the database to administering the right medication, there is a process that can be established and followed to make certain that patients are safeguarded in our care. Removing defects in work processes is likely your best effort in promoting patient safety.

Waste 7: Overproduction

Overproduction means doing more work than necessary. Just one example, redundant paperwork, is likely a crisis in itself in the healthcare industry! The waste of patient time and possibility of error when hastily answering duplicate questions is something we have all experienced. That waste is many times compounded with the worker time and potential errors in interpreting sometimes conflicting records. Automatic reporting of useless information to administration and regulatory agencies likewise eats up time and dollars. And paperwork is just one form of overproduction in healthcare.

Doing too much when just enough meets the demand is apparent in many healthcare systems. Although we would never negate the value of a compassionate touch or a kind word, most patients report that they want exactly what is needed to get them in and out of hospital services—no less, no more. Compassion and caring can be combined (and likely enhanced!) by removing needless activities from healthcare processes.

Summary

No worker, particularly in healthcare, where the well-being and safety of another human is the core of the work, appreciates having his or her time wasted. Recognizing sources of *muda* in daily work is the first step in eliminating waste, and eliminating waste is the first step in recognizing the value in a worker's time well spent. When healthcare workers look at their work with a keener eye for measuring value, the healthcare environment transforms to a safer, more affordable network for health management.

As organizations institutionalize the philosophies of improving quality and safety, and capitalize on every employee's contribution of waste reduction, robust healthcare business environments can be created. Success in the healthcare marketplace comes around full circle to offer even better and more timely service to the patients who depend so faithfully on your care.

References

Jimmerson, C., D. Weber, and D. Sobek. 2005. Reducing waste and errors: Piloting lean principles at Intermountain Healthcare. *Journal on Quality and Patient Safety* 31(5):249–257.

Tucker, A. L., and S. J. Spear. 2006. Operational failures and interruptions in hospital nursing. *Health Resources Research* 41(3):643–662.

Chapter 2

The Ideal State in Healthcare

Perhaps the most powerful notion credited to Toyota's success is their relentless efforts toward an *ideal state*. Building off the definition of Anita Tucker and Steven Spear of an ideal state for Toyota, consider the following ideal state for healthcare:

- **Defect-free delivery:** Exactly what the patient needs
- **No waste in the system:** None of the seven *mudas* discussed in Chapter 1 is present
- **Individual attention to patients:** One-on-one care that is customized to each patient
- **On-demand healthcare:** Care that is exactly as requested, when requested
- **Immediate response to problems:** A safer environment for patients and workers, with no replication of recognized problems

Let us consider these characteristics of an ideal system one at a time.

Defect-Free Delivery

Any essential service like healthcare (and also public transportation, law enforcement, primary education) would like to be able to claim that its product or service is defect free. As consumers of services, we would love to be confident that the service we receive (and pay for!) is indeed without defects. But as we all know from our own painful experiences, from the airlines delivering luggage to the correct destination to healthcare creating accurate bills, defect free is not a norm in service industries. In any service industry, you can easily recall examples of receiving the service that was requested, but only after a journey that was complex, time-consuming, and that perhaps involved correcting real or near errors along the way.

I love the term "defect free," because it says so much more than "right" or "wrong." Defect free suggests a level of superiority beyond "good enough;" it suggests that healthcare service has to be produced without a single problem along the way to delivery.

A product or service without defects, particularly in industries such as healthcare, will produce significantly improved outcomes over a defective service. The apparent results of better care and satisfaction of the patient and dramatic scores in worker satisfaction will be measurable. The cost of producing defect-free care to patients can be quantified not only in happy, returning customers, but in the cost of remediation of errors and redundant activities by the labor force.

No Waste in the System

Together with near-perfect quality, the hallmark of the Toyota Production System (TPS) is constant attention to eliminating waste from all aspects of their production and service. Waste in its most basic definition includes anything that does not add value to the customer/patient or to the process. (See Chapter 1 for details.) Consequently when you observe work in healthcare, it should be with an eye toward identifying any activity that impairs or delays value, both to the patient/customer and to the worker providing the service.

Individual Attention to Patients

As the world community becomes more homogenous, it is easy to globalize service and assume that similar patients will require the same level and detail of care. On the contrary, the concept of each patient or customer as an individual must be kept at the forefront of delivering ideal service. Although mass production, whether of cars or flu shots, may appear to be the most practical and cost-effective method of delivering care, truly ideal service has to include attention to the requirements of each individual. Without such a laser focus on each customer or patient, you will likely need workarounds and rework that complicate and delay the delivery of care, and will certainly lead to additional expense.

The point here is not to *avoid* standardizing work processes, but rather to implicate the importance of designing standardized processes that support flexibility in professional care, and that, in turn, enhance individual attention to specific needs. An ideal state developed without a focus on treating each patient as a unique entity would cripple each caregiver from delivering truly ideal care.

On-Demand Healthcare

In the last 40 years in America (and around the world), fast-food restaurants have changed the way we eat by perfecting one element of ideal: on demand. Think about it, we drive up, give our exact order (which varies with each customer) through a speaker system, while in line behind other cars in the next steps of the process. Then we pay at the first window (their accounts receivable is measured in seconds, not in weeks and months) and collect exactly what we ordered at the last window. And we never have to find a parking place, stand in line, or eat food that sat under a heat lamp for hours.

As an industry that spends millions of dollars every year building, remodeling, and furnishing waiting rooms and parking garages, perhaps healthcare has something to learn from the hamburger industry! It is time that we think outside of our familiar boundaries and consider delivering on-demand service. Picking up our prescriptions at a drive-through pharmacy is one example of how this trend is changing. But why cannot we also get our cholesterol checked at a drive-through lab or store our medical records on a magnetic strip?

Giving customers exactly what they want, when they want it, is a core principle of an ideal state. As you observe work in progress, note the delays in care created by caregivers waiting for necessities from their suppliers (e.g., a nurse waiting for the delivery of a medication from the pharmacy). It is easy to see the delay passed on to the patient and the cost passed on to the organization.

Immediate Response to Problems

For process improvement to succeed, it is imperative to recognize when a process is *not* working and clearly understand procedures for correction. Succinctly defining what is expected of a system allows workers to easily recognize when defects occur and triggers an immediate response to that failure. For example, if information related to dietary allergies is obtained from a patient but not communicated as part of the food preparation process, meals could come off the tray line with potentially hazardous components. In most hospitals, there is a clear mechanism for determining diet specifications for every admitted patient. If no specific diet order exists for a patient, the process must alert the dietary staff to confirm the diet order before preparing the meal. But only if the process has a clear signal to alert the staff to aberrations or failures can you trust it! A perfect process is one that is designed to not allow the worker to do the work incorrectly; this should be a goal with all process design.

Immediate responses to problems identified by the people doing the work prevent the regeneration of defective work. It also initiates the improvement that sets a thinking organization apart from the more traditional command-and-control management. Ideally no defect or problem would occur more than once, and in its correction another layer of learning will have occurred.

A Safe Work Environment

Continuous improvement and innovation can only occur when parameters for patient and worker safety exist. This "safety" includes not just avoidance of physical risk, but confidence that suggestions for improvement and "out of the box" thinking will be respected and encouraged. No participants of healthcare should feel that their position in the organization is in jeopardy when they contribute ideas to process improvement.

The culture of any organization (which I interpret simply as "how we work here") will ideally create a safe ground for process improvement and innovation. Lean thinking and the concept tools of value stream mapping and A3 problem solving support the desired culture because they produce objective information, never assigning blame. Focusing on process weakness and not on personal or departmental failure motivates workers to expose problems so that they can be eliminated. The only truly dangerous problem is the one that is swept under the carpet and not exposed for correction. Organizational culture must celebrate those exposures as opportunities for improvement.

Summary

The state of ideal may appear to be lofty—goals you consider unachievable 100% of the time. However, harboring the elements of ideal as the destination toward which to strive creates a consistent goal. You can measure adherence to this goal both in terms of strategic moves in the organization and in simple tasks of individual work.

When considering any proposal to change a policy or practice ask, "Will the proposed activities move us closer to ideal?" If the answer is a resounding "Yes!", it is not difficult to move forward with confidence. If the proposal does not move the organization toward ideal, you can usually get a clear indication of where the proposal falls short on one of the points. Adjusting the proposal toward an ideal outcome is straightforward with specific direction for redesign.

Chapter 3

Adapting the Four Rules in Use to Healthcare Processes

Chapter 2 puts the golden egg—the ideal state—in sight. But how do you get there? In 1999, Steven Spear interpreted four rules he observed at Toyota that enable workers to create and maintain processes that move them closer and closer to ideal. Those four rules apply directly to the work of almost any organization, and are particularly relevant to healthcare. All processes and activities in the daily delivery of care can be assessed against the four rules reviewed in this chapter.

Rule 1: Clearly Specify All Activities of Work

Rule 1 states that the activities of work within a process should be clearly defined as to what should happen, in what order they should occur, and how long the activities should take to complete. It also states that the outcome or goal of the work must be absolutely clear to the people doing the work.

In healthcare, violation of this rule is frequently the source of confusion, errors, and the general discomfort of healthcare workers. Perhaps because healthcare is a well-educated workforce, the unspoken expectation has been that each worker will figure out processes that support their work; that is, that they should not require daily activities to be clearly defined. This assumption frequently leads to several different workers doing the same bit of work in different ways. Overlapping work of this sort can create misconceptions about what tasks have been done and what should happen at various steps along the way, such as when patient care is transferred from one caregiver to another, when patients are discharged, and even when bills are created for services rendered. Specifying (or another way to say this is, "standardizing") the work is never intended to interfere with professional judgment. On the contrary, it is there to build confidence and reliability in processes that support good work.

A clear example of this rule in action is ordering laboratory studies for a patient in the emergency department (ED). Every ED nurse, clerk, or physician may place the order differently than his or her peers if the steps in the process are not clearly defined. Some may order through computerized order entry or e-mail, some may call on the phone, some may pass a paper order through a delivery system, some may deliver paperwork personally, and some may stop the person in the course of work and make a verbal request.

The request form may give more information than necessary for the test to be conducted, or it may be missing some pieces of information. The request may be delivered at the wrong time, to the wrong location, or to the wrong person. And expectations of the time in which the results of the test will be available may be completely unclear, which leads to unnecessary phone calls in search of test results. Even details as seemingly meaningless as where the results are delivered can create confusion and delay if the information does not get to the right person, on time, every time. The actual processing of the lab specimen may be flawed and inconsistent. Some technicians may process and report the results differently than others.

When any process is examined, the following questions (and many more) might be asked:

- Is it clear what should happen, in what order, and is there an approximate time frame for completion?
- Is every step in the current process adding value to the patient?
- Is the participation of every person who touches the process necessary?
- Does everyone who uses this process do it the same way?
- How does a new worker learn this process?
- How did *you* learn this process?
- About how long should it take for the process to complete?
- Is the expected outcome clearly understood?
- What is the expected outcome?

Answers to these kinds of questions illuminate the strengths and weaknesses of the process and contribute to ideas for redesigning the work.

As you begin to clearly specify work activities, listen for the "bad words" that you will quickly grow to relate to fingernails on a blackboard, the ones that point clearly to an inconsistent and unreliable process. Here are a few of those words:

- Sometimes
- Maybe
- If
- It depends
- Possibly
- Perhaps

Also look for the classic answer to the question, "Why do we do it this way?" which is, of course, "Because we've always done it this way!"

Rule 2: All Steps In a Request for a Product or Service Are Simple and Direct

This rule points to the complexity and variety of ways that a service or product can be requested. The goal is that the request process be simple (i.e., with as few steps as possible) and direct (i.e., the requestor gets as close as possible to the person who can offer the service or deliver the product).

Consider this familiar example to illustrate when Rule 2 is *not* happening: You call a business 800 number and get a telephone menu. If (and that is a big if) you listen carefully and the choices are clear, you make a selection on your phone that takes you one layer closer to the outcome you want. This can continue for 2, 3, even 10 times before you get what you want. And that is if you are listening closely and the choices are obvious. Should you become confused and push the wrong button, misunderstand the choice offered, or (horrors!) be disconnected, your request could go on forever.

In 2004, 100 billion calls were made to toll free numbers. Think of your last frustrating experience calling one of those numbers and multiply it by 100 billion. If we could only harness the energy of that frustration, we could easily eliminate our dependency on foreign oil. (Could we measure the "frustration" in the millimeters of mercury that our blood pressures rises?) Incidentally, I frequently use this example to illustrate complex connections in classes and ask the participants the same question every time: What do you really want? Their replies, without exception, have been the same every time: I wanted to talk to a human. Hmm…makes you wonder if somewhere along the line the developers of telephone menus took their eyes off the objective and created a process that worked for them and not the customer (see Figure 3.1).

When studying healthcare processes, for those we assumed were broken, the *requests* for those services are often as complex and unreliable as the actual steps of producing the requested product or service. The complexity of some request processes is staggering, and observation of the way a service is requested can reveal some real surprises.

In examining the steps in a request, the number of connections between people is a clear indication of the complexity of the requesting process. Ideally all connections are as direct as possible, with few steps and few people involved in relaying the request. Likewise, if the system is working optimally, all users of the process will request that process in the exact same way. This will make the progress of the request transparent—in other words, at any given time, the staff will have a sound understanding of how long it should be until the request is filled and where the activity is in the request process. The incidence of error related

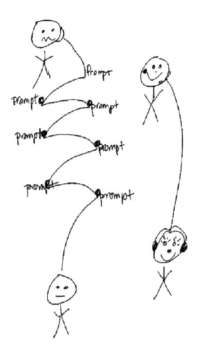

Figure 3.1

to missed or delayed requests will go down by a factor of the number of options that are eliminated. And time wasted calling to confirm receipt of requests and looking for results before the expected time will be reduced. Related to our lab example above, the system of requesting lab tests will be solid and the staff will have confidence that it will work every time.

When you first go out to observe a process, be certain to investigate the "request" portion of the process before you do anything else. Always look as far upstream (as close to the requestor) as possible to identify the first snafu. If the request does not flow without interruptions, it will likely also generate problems in the pathway of activities needed to deliver the requested outcome. Correcting the problems furthest upstream can yield more improvement than may be assumed on first blush.

Rule 3: The Flow of Steps Required to Deliver a Request Is Simple and Direct

The delivery of the requested product or service should involve as few steps and as few people as possible, always working toward the ideal state. For example, when a specimen reaches a laboratory, you want to look carefully at the steps and hands that the specimen passes through to completion, as well as the delays and sources of delay (traveling, in queues, unnecessary processing, worker handoffs, and so on) to identify opportunities to eliminate any wasted time or unnecessary activities.

The goal is to use as few steps and as few people as possible to produce the highest possible quality. By reviewing the detailed activities within each step, it will be easy to recognize redundant work and opportunities to reduce handoffs between workers. Each activity within a step needs to pass the following test to determine inclusion in a perfect process: Is this activity necessary to produce an ideal outcome? It should be easy to answer the question with a yes or no. If the "bad words" from Rule 1 ("sometimes," "maybe," "depends," "if," and so on) come into the answer, that process can use some help.

Rule 4: All Problems Are Addressed Directly and In a Timely Way, Under the Guidance of a Coach

The final rule ensures that no error, once identified, will be allowed to be repeated. In this rule lies the recognition of the people doing the work as the most appropriate individuals to solve a problem. It also establishes the expectation that an experienced problem-solving coach, who has designated time outside the delivery of care, will be available to assist when a problem needs to be addressed.

In an ideal state, the processes of work abide by Rules 1, 2, and 3, and thus are transparent enough to expose when one of those rules is violated. Rule 4 says it is now time to

- Figure out why one of the first three rules has failed.
- Take care of it, as soon as possible after the event, involving the people doing the work.

In order for this rule to be used to its maximum effect, you must have a way to look at process failures that will quickly and objectively expose where the failure occurred. The process, thinking, and documents that are created with value stream mapping and A3 problem solving achieve high-level and detailed scrutiny that enable Rule 4. Having one common way to address process failure in an organization is as important as the method itself. As you move into the next chapter and start to understand how value stream mapping works, I am confident that you will begin to recall occasions in your work history when this approach to vexing and unsafe processes could have saved suffering for your patients and for the staff at your location.

Summary

The four rules discussed in this chapter are the standards by which you can measure the elements of your work. If communicating, producing, and improving the work are not clear, simple, and well defined, weaknesses will occur. As you break down the activities of work through value stream mapping (see Chapter 4), you can easily weigh each part for clarity, simplicity, and directness. These four rules alone will not do the job, nor will only the concept of an ideal state, nor will a value stream map, but together they make evaluation of your healthcare system pragmatic, objective, and fair.

Chapter 4

Value Stream Mapping the Work of Healthcare

The term value stream map (VSM) refers to a graphic representation of the trail of activities that occur from the moment a request is made for a service or product until the moment that request is satisfied. You will be creating these simple maps, using pencil and paper, in an attempt to move your healthcare organization toward a zero-waste, ideal state.

Each of the steps in a VSM indicates when something is done to get closer to completion of any request. The addition of simple data creates a time and motion study of what is happening that adds to or subtracts value from the requestor. The operative word in the term is *value*. You create VSMs to better understand and evaluate the processes of daily work, but the ability to see and measure each of the steps for its true value—through the eyes of the requestor—is the essence of this method. In objectively evaluating the steps for value, clarifying what does not add value pinpoints what activities can be eliminated in the process; clarifying what does add value pinpoints what should remain in the process. In this recognition is the opportunity to remove non-value-adding steps and eliminate waste. As you eliminate waste, you increase capacity, decrease worker frustration, and most importantly, develop a means for quicker, safer delivery of the care a patient requires.

Why You Need Value Stream Mapping

Value stream mapping offers a high-level view of the steps and activities in a process and allows you to recognize where there are areas of concern (and opportunity) on which you can focus your problem-solving resources. Because VSMs are drawn with a pencil, they can be modified in scope to fit the "scope" requirements of any group that is interested in improving a process. For example,

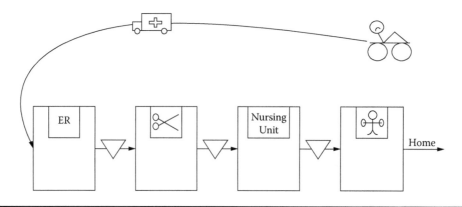

Figure 4.1

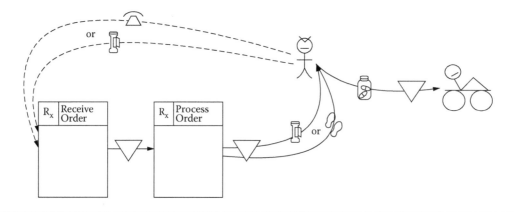

Figure 4.2

for organizational planners and administrators, the views may be very high, with greater scope but less detail. For a nurse or technician at the bedside, the details on the map may be finer and the scope much narrower to address a particular process of specific work.

Consider Figure 4.1 as a view from 100,000 feet and Figure 4.2 as a view from 10,000 feet. In both cases it is easy to see the steps in the request and the steps required to complete the request, and the information obtained is pertinent to the map creators.

VSMs are sometimes referred to as tools, but the mapping method is more than that. Value stream maps are a fundamental component of the Toyota Production System (TPS/Lean) that allows you to deeply understand processes so that work can be adjusted to increase value to the customer, eliminate waste, and reach the ideal state. The process works like this:

1. Value stream maps provide elemental information obtained by direct observation from which specific problem solving is directed.
2. In turn, A3 problem solving reveals opportunities to use lean methods to maximize flow and improve quality.
3. Value stream maps provide visual and transparent interpretations of work that contribute essential information for achieving organizational goals. This

reaches every work level of the organization and begins to weave the fabric of innovation that has made the Toyota Motor Company so iconic.

VSMs are created from a combination of historical knowledge and direct observation; that is, value stream maps can be done from memory, with direct observation being the validating step that highlights any inaccuracies or short-comings. Observing each process keeps the information in the map objective and accurate and is the first step toward process improvement.

The easy-to-learn and easy-to-teach method of value stream mapping looks at both the steps in the request process and the steps in producing that requested service. It is amazing how much complexity can be identified in the activities of making a request! Because the request occurs upstream (i.e., at or near the beginning) in the overall process, specifying the steps and simplifying this part of the process can often positively affect the operations downstream. Likewise, understanding and validating the activities within each step required to answer a request expose redundancy and inconsistency and inspire clear ideas for improvement. Validation of the map with the people who do the work offers two critical elements of process improvement: *accuracy* and *buy-in from the staff.*

The Anatomy of a Value Stream Map

A value stream map is a graphic representation of the steps in a request for a product or service, as well as the steps required to answer that request. It is ini-tially hand drawn with pencil on a piece of 11 inch × 17 inch (also known as A3 size) paper. As you improve your mapping skills, you will also want to use VSMs in meetings, in which whiteboards and colored markers take the technique to another scale of speed, changeability, and communication clarity. Always remem-ber, however, to have someone create a pencil-and-paper copy to take from the meeting for preservation and portability.

Layout, Title, Date, and Names

Every value stream map, whether the map is of the current or future state (see Chapters 6 and 7, respectively), needs to have a title, a date, and the names or initials of the key people involved with its composition. The title information, as shown in Figure 4.3, should be placed in the upper right-hand corner of the sheet on which it is drawn. Then, with a simple half fold on itself and a right-side

Lab Request from MD

Date: June 26, 2007
By: AJ, CJ, DA

Figure 4.3

Lab Request from MD
Date: June 26, 2007
By AJ, CJ, DA

Figure 4.4

quarter fold back, the title, date, and owner information will be revealed, and the paper-drawn document can be kept in a ring binder for easy storage and the title information will be easy to reference.

It is easiest to divide your value stream map into three horizontal sections:

- The upper third is occupied by the requestor and the steps that comprise the request.
- The center section is for the process steps in answering the request.
- The bottom third is for the compilation of related data.

As shown in Figure 4.4, the person making the request is drawn as a stick figure (or stick figures, if a group is represented) to be placed on the right side of the paper, in the upper third portion.

Upper Third: Steps That Comprise the Request

Indicating how the request for a product or service is made is the first (and sometimes the most enlightening) step in understanding a process. Unlike a conventional flowchart, wherein you might map how work is *intended* to happen, with value stream mapping you chart every step as it *really* happens and each way that it may be communicated. As in the example in Figure 4.5, if sometimes the request for a lab study is called to the lab by phone, an arrow from the

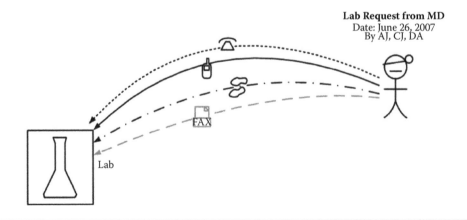

Figure 4.5

doctor's office would be drawn to the lab, with a simple phone drawn above it. If a similar request is sometimes faxed, another arrow is drawn from the office to the lab with a fax icon drawn above it. If a worker sometimes stops a lab technician in person and requests the test, that would be drawn as well. Obviously as you put down on paper all the possible ways that the request can be made, the complexity of the requesting process becomes clear and it is easy to see why a clearly specified process for submitting a request could make the work more reliable. Potential communication failure is easy to spot.

Associated with each additional and perhaps ambiguous method of requesting is a risk for the request to be lost, delayed, or misunderstood. Your goal with any process improvement work is to create processes that work consistently and reliably. The top third of the value stream map will reveal the often complicated and redundant steps involved with initiating the delivery of a product or service. The understanding and awareness of that complexity in turn generates ideas for simplifying and standardizing a preferred request process.

Frequently in the work of healthcare delivery, the department from which a request is made is not the department that produces the result. When a request process fails, for example, when the request is not received on time or accurately, the unhealthy tendency is for one department to blame another for the failure. Instead of asking why the system failed, a person or group may be faulted. When the steps for a request are included on the map, the realization that the system (or lack of a clearly defined one) has faults is visibly clear and objective, and the associated departments can tackle an improvement from a safe place of cooperation instead of blaming. It has been very interesting to watch once-opposing departments team up with a common purpose of improving the work as the process problems are revealed in a safe context. It has been even more amazing to watch busy workers offer additional effort to make a system work better after they have seen how their own actions fit into the big picture of the process.

Note: Sometimes the request for a specific service is inferred by adjacent activities and there are no steps to draw. In this rare case, a single arrow from the requestor to the beginning of the process boxes is drawn with an explanatory word over the arrow, as in Figure 4.6.

The point of creating a visual document is to use the power of the image for understanding. Limit the use of words to necessary clarification and use familiar

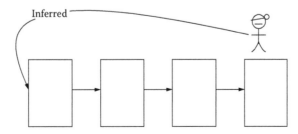

Figure 4.6

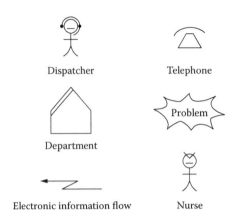

Dispatcher

Telephone

Department

Problem

Electronic information flow

Nurse

Figure 4.7

Legend

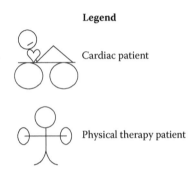

Cardiac patient

Physical therapy patient

Figure 4.8

icons when possible. (See Figure 4.7 for a few sample icons.) If it makes sense to create icons for specific activities or people involved, keep them simple and draw a simple legend in the upper left corner of the map, as shown in Figure 4.8.

Center Third: Steps Deliver the Requested Product or Service

Once the request has been received and the steps, icons, and arrows have been indicated from the requestor, the necessary steps required for delivering results are also mapped, this time in the center third of the map. As with the request, the process is mapped from the left, parallel to the steps in the request, but headed back to the right side.

The steps are drawn as vertical rectangles, with titles on the top of each box. These are called *process boxes*, and one is drawn for each major step in the process. There are likely many activities that occur inside each process box to create that step, and depending on the detail that you are seeking in the mapping exercise and the intended use of the map, you may choose to write the activities in each box in the order in which they occur. Think of the boxes as having doors. Ask yourself, what is the first activity that opens the door to this process box and what is the last activity that closes the door on that step? When you begin adding data to the boxes, it is critical to be certain that the data you are collecting is accurate and that your understanding is shared and sound.

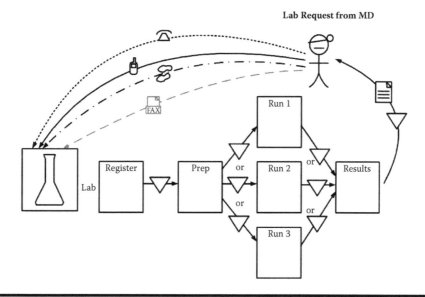

Figure 4.9

Remember that the point of mapping is to obtain a deep understanding of how the work happens now (current state map—see Chapter 5) and how we intend it to happen when improvements are engaged (future state map—see Chapter 6). As with the steps in the request, the process boxes are strung together in order of occurrence with arrows that indicate a path to the next step. Sometimes there are divergent options for steps, and each optional process box is drawn as though stacked, with arrows labeled "or" to indicate a selection (see Figure 4.9). After such a divergence, the flow of activities usually converges into one stream.

If too much complexity begins to appear on the map, it is a signal to reevaluate the map and consider if it might be too big and that better information might be obtained if it were made more specific. For example, a process may greatly differ on the night shift compared to the same process on the day shift. Mapping all the different options that may occur but are not specific to either days or nights will likely make the map confusing and difficult to read. Two separate maps—one indicating the flow for the night shift and one for the day shift—will be easier to read, will be relevant to each shift, and will clearly highlight the differences in the activities of each shift. It is also much quicker and easier to draw a process that has fewer variables.

In addition to the deep understanding that can be garnered from the process box information, the recognition of when nothing is happening to move the process along is equally valuable information. This non-value-added time is represented by an inverted triangle (called a delta), and is best included as an icon of different color (red stands out nicely) or as a solid color when black and white is the only option. When a request is sitting in an inbox, when a lab specimen is waiting to be processed, when a dinner tray is waiting to be delivered, no value is being added to the person who requested it. This is waste. Non-value-added time is an opportunity waiting to be capitalized on.

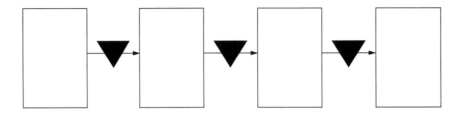

Figure 4.10

On the map, this delta is drawn interrupting the arrow that indicates the flow from process box to process box (see Figure 4.10). These interruptions are significant as you use the map to evaluate the flow of the work, but they offer even more information when the actual time spent in the deltas (waiting) is measured, along with the value-adding activities.

Comparing the time spent adding value (the process boxes) and time spent adding no value (the deltas) can create a frightening revelation. It is amazing how much time is consumed by tasks that you accept as part of the work, but in reality add no real value to your patients or to the work of your organization. This lack of worth in work is perceived by caregivers and patients alike, and tends to be exhibited as frustration. Only good can come from eliminating as much non-value-adding activity as possible.

Bottom Third: Compiling Related Data

Data are collated on the bottom third of a value stream map to add another layer of understanding beyond what you see initially related to the flow of work activities. Although this data compilation does not have to be lengthy, it adds objectivity and emphasis to the assumptions you would develop by looking at flow alone. Data also answer questions that normally arise when looking at processes, such as the following:

- Does it take the same time to produce a step (represented by process boxes) every time; if not, what is the least amount of time, the greatest amount of time, and the average time consumed by each step?
- Do delays (represented by deltas) take the same amount of time; if not, what is the least, most, and average delay between steps?
- Relative to the time spent in process boxes, what percent of the total time consumed by the process is non-value-added?

Information like this often leads to a number of other questions, most of which start with "why" and are all good questions in the discovery of the root cause of process problems.

Highlights of a Well-Drawn Value Stream Map

When you reflect on a completed value stream map, certain features will contribute to inuring staff to the concept of process improvement. Here are a few features of a successful value stream map:

- It tells the story of a process on its own or can be easily explained by the authors.
- The process is specific enough to create a succinct story.
- The writing is legible.
- The map and data fill the entire 11 inch × 17 inch (or A3) paper.
- The title information is complete.
- The request is easily recognized as separate from the process boxes.
- Process boxes each contain similar or uninterrupted activities.
- The data line up and are easy to correlate with the associated boxes/deltas.
- Color is used to separate information when needed.
- Lines and arrows are labeled with icons or words only as needed for clarification.

Well-drawn value stream maps, which are done only with pencil and paper, are a thing of beauty, but an electronic version is helpful for sharing, projecting, or archiving good maps. Please refer to the discussion in Chapter 8 of expanded opportunities for creating electronic versions of your pencil-drawn value stream maps.

What You Can Do With a Value Stream Map

So this clever pencil-drawn map can be effective in initiating a change in the way you do your work. What else can it do—what else can you do with the information, the layout, and the design of this foundation of work? The following are a few ideas:

- Project planning and reporting
- High-level strategizing
- Aligning improvements with the strategic plan
- Training (visual aids for orienting new hires and existing staff to a process)
- Patient education
- Explaining procedures to patients
- Demonstrating/documenting improvements to regulatory agencies
- Communicating change between departments
- Initiating new policies
- Replacing or augmenting policy manuals

Value stream mapping provides a methodical way of looking deeply at the activities of work and allows management and staff to really know how work happens here. I believe that this is the way you define the culture of any organization: "how work happens here." Value stream maps give you a picture of how your work flows and enables you to make peace with that flow by removing obstacles, interruptions, and delays in daily work. This results in fewer errors, lower operating costs, and much less worker frustration. It results in more scientific and compassionate time with patients and more patients being served. By improving how work happens here, you build the trust of your community and the loyalty of your workforce.

Summary

A simple but succinct definition of ideal for any organization, work unit, or specific activity or service acts as a beacon toward which staff can move their work. Even the activity of doing the defining builds consensus and initiates participation. Using value stream mapping to understand work in progress and applying the four rules to analyze that work are the first steps toward ideal. This is a roadmap that can be applied to any work, at any level, in any organization. The flexibility of TPS/Lean is demonstrated with the endless opportunities in which staff and leadership can make effective change when these concepts are embraced and exercised.

Chapter 5

Creating and Using Your First Map

The Current State

A value stream map charts the current state—that is, it is an objective, data-supported bank of information that offers a clear window from which to see the way work really happens right now, from the initial request to the completion of the work. The current state map tells you in which order each step of the process occurs, how long each step takes for completion, and the delays between each step. It allows you to see how the work steps flow and where there are interruptions to that flow. Ideally (see Chapter 7 for information on the future state map), all work would flow from beginning to end with no interruptions or delays in that course. Information about the specific activities completed in each step of the current state is added for further clarification, as needed.

As discussed in earlier chapters, the current state map is drawn by hand on plain 11 inch × 17 inch (A3) paper and is a very flexible tool. It can be used to understand processes from a very high level or to analyze a specific process that occurs within a greater scheme. The flexibility of value stream mapping makes it applicable to any environment where a request is made for goods or services. Information obtained by direct observation and formatted in this way creates a very easy to understand base for deep comprehension of the work.

The rules for creating a current state map are simple, but creating it demands some rigor:

- The map can be finalized only when the entire process has been directly observed; you must "walk" the process to verify the accuracy of the flow of work.
- The current state map must be validated by the people who do the work, both for accuracy and to generate ideas and buy-in for upcoming improvements.

The tendency in most people is to assume that we know how work happens based on our experience and familiarity with the process. The natural next step would be to rely on this information alone (instead of verifying it) and come up with an improvement. Unfortunately when we give in to this tendency, many opportunities can be missed, so that fatal, albeit subtle, errors occur. The current state map requires you to scrutinize a process bit by bit. The transparency of the work as it is mapped reveals opportunities to correct or simplify the work that you may have otherwise overlooked.

Knowing Whom to Involve

So where should you start, and who should create and contribute to the mapping process? The easy answer is, "start everywhere and include everybody!" Although that is not practical in a large, complex organization, the goal from the start should revolve around eventual participation of all staff affected by the work. That's right: All staff. In healthcare organizations, that span will include the CEO, housekeepers, intensive care unit (ICU) nurses, lab technicians, nutritionists…you get the point. This is not an isolated activity of the quality department!

Every time a request is made for a product or service, a value stream map can be drawn. So it is easy to ask yourself, What requests were made of me today? What steps did I have to follow to answer that request? How many coworkers contributed to the result? Visualizing a map of those steps, no matter how simple or complex, will give you a whole new appreciation of the exhaustion you feel at the end of a hectic day!

Note: There should be one person—and only one person—responsible for drawing a value stream map and for compiling and reporting the information on it. All the contributors of information should submit ideas and data through a single facilitator for each map.

Starting With the Front Line

Lean has been touted as being effective because improvement occurs where the work happens, at the front line. And although that is exactly true, administrators may assume that the front line refers only to the bedside, the lab counter, or the tray assembly kitchen. The truth is that we all have frontline work. One of the objectives of my research (along with coinvestigator Durward Sobek) (NSF grant 0115352, Applying the principles of the Toyota Production System to healthcare, 2000–2002) was to apply lean thinking in every department of the hospital, not just in the most sophisticated ICU or most technically advanced radiology department. The objective of organization-wide application was met, with remarkably similar results (and challenges) in every department, including the administrative suite.

Defining "Front Line"

You could define frontline work as the work done day by day to accomplish the expectations of each job. Hence, for the hospital CEO, the complex responsibility of hiring a new physician could be the subject of a value stream map. How is the request made for physician applicants? What are the steps in advertising, interviewing, and negotiating a contract? How many steps are involved? How much time passes between steps when nothing is happening? Do all the steps add value to the new doctor, the hospital, and the process? Could the same objectives be met with fewer steps and perhaps fewer people or less time?

Figure 5.1 shows a completed value stream map. If you refer to this document as you progress through the book, each of the aggregated parts will take on deeper significance.

Likewise, if an overhead light burns out in the operating room, a VSM could be drawn to show the process for sending a stat work order to plant maintenance for its replacement and all the activities that are required to repair the essential light.

In both of these situations, more than one entity will need to be engaged in creating an accurate map. A collaborative advantage of using a pencil to draw the first value stream map is that it ensures easy validating with the other affected parties. The on-the-spot changeability of a pencil-drawn document allows for completeness, accuracy, and involvement of the people who will use the changed

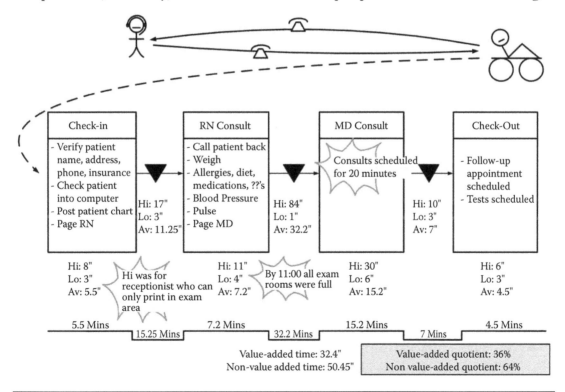

Figure 5.1

process (and whose good ideas should be mined). In addition, by using colored markers and whiteboards to create maps that show the flow of a product (or patient), the workers involved can clarify a previously vague interpretation of a piece of work. Groups of related stakeholders from different departments can walk away from otherwise laborious meetings with a concise understanding of the current state and the plan to move toward improvement. And this can happen in any department, with a view from any scope. The common misunderstanding about where lean concepts and activities can be applied is likely the biggest reason organizations stumble in their initial implementation efforts. Only when every member of an organization realizes the advantages of adding value and reducing waste in his or her own work will Toyota-like results be achieved.

Preparing Everyone Involved

Be sure to prepare every worker and patient being observed. They must know that this observation is not a criticizing or punitive event, but that the observer is looking at the process with an eye on improvement, which will ultimately improve the work environment and help them. The workers being observed need to be actively engaged in the observation, not to interrupt their work, but for them to be mindful of and signal to the observer small interruptions or variations in the process as the observation progresses. These subtle nuances will both enrich the information on the map and initiate worker interest and buy-in for improving the process.

When information on the finished map is evaluated, you will be looking for roadblocks in the work that make the times in a process box or a delta (delay) unnecessarily long. The contribution of these details by the workers themselves creates consciousness raising about work that they may have accepted as normal for a long time without questioning or may validate frustration they have felt with the work.

Factors That Point to a Good First Team

Like introducing anything new, there are some factors that make choosing an initial improvement team less risky and more likely to demonstrate successful change. Here are a few conditions to consider when choosing a team:

■ Local management is informed about the process and expectations and eager to think outside the box and try something new.
■ Staffing is reasonably stable.
■ You have physician support, if this is a clinical area or process. (It is essential to not leave physicians out of the process improvement activities. If their work will be affected by the process, they need to be involved and thought

of as all other staff. With just one good experience they become priceless advocates of this work to their peers. Never underestimate the power of informal chats in the doctors' lounge.)

■ You have a stable environment, meaning no other large initiatives are being introduced simultaneous to the improvement work. This includes construction, remodeling, information technology (IT) systems changes, and so on.

■ Someone from the administrative team will "own" the efforts. This is someone who really knows the unit and is willing to be there with the workers, observing, listening, and attending work sessions. This person is also a critical link to the CEO's administrative team who will need to be kept abreast of the progress of the work, may need to approve systemic changes beyond the local authority of the manager/director, will remove administrative roadblocks for the changes required, and, of course, may appropriate funds and staff time for extended improvements when justified.

Mapping the First Process

When choosing the first process to map, consider the following:

■ The process must be observable; in other words, it must be a process that can be followed and for which results can be seen.

■ For the sake of accelerating observations, data collection and testing changes, it is best if the process occurs frequently. Observing a process that arises only once or twice a month may have value, but it is likely not a good place to start. One of the most gratifying features of lean efforts is that they are quick and results can be seen and understood while the work is fresh.

■ The process must be recognized by the staff and the administrative team as worthy of the resources being dedicated to the improvement efforts. Establishing the importance to the customer (patient), the organization, and the worker is critical in determining its worth.

Observing the Process

The act of observing is worthy in its own right. Really looking at work in motion, particularly when you are watching with fresh, focused eyes, is an opportunity to really truly see the details of work. Only rarely does one big problem create waste and errors in a process; instead, many seemingly insignificant delays and missteps compile and become hazards. You can identify those nuggets of opportunity only if you take the time to engage in the practice of observation.

When observing a process for the first time, there are a number of steps to take and key questions and considerations:

1. Identify the first activity in initiating the process.
   - Who made the request?
   - How was the request generated, and what was each step that followed?
   - How many handoffs occurred in the request?

2. Draw the details into the first map, including value-added process boxes and non-value-added time and wait times (deltas).
   - Draw process boxes to indicate each major step. Remember that the activities within the box should be similar or sequential activities that together accomplish the step that you define with a title (e.g., registration is a definable step in a patient visit that can be represented by a process box; within that box there are likely many activities required to complete the registration). Even though you may recognize some waste within each box, for the current state map (CSM), the activities that are required *now* to complete the step are all considered value added because they are necessary for the process as it currently works.
   - Title each process box.
   - Indicate the time when nothing is happening to move the process along between process boxes with deltas. This is waste!

3. Validate each rendition of the map with the people who do the work. It is very important to approach the workers with a humble attitude and a healthy eraser in hand and ask:
   - Does this look right to you?
   - Did I leave anything out?
   - Is there something we need to change to make it accurate or more complete?

The beauty of drawing this with pencil (or on a whiteboard) is that you can erase and correct it immediately when information needs to be added or changed.

Keep in mind that you do not want to mix apples and oranges on one map. Be specific about the requested service or item. If requesting a hot meal after a patient returns from surgery has different steps and activities than ordering a hot meal for a newly admitted patient in rehab, do not try to put these two different processes on the same map. Two unique maps that address how the work currently happens in these different situations will greatly increase the effectiveness and accuracy of upcoming changes and the credibility of your efforts with the staff. Generalizing problems and diluting the significance of details is a death sentence for process improvement.

As a caveat to that, when a CSM is created for one process, for instance getting a hot meal for a post-op patient, much of the learning will be applicable to a similar process (getting a hot meal for a newly admitted patient in rehab) and with that learning each related map will progress with less work and more speed.

Evaluating the Map for Completeness and Accuracy

Because it is so important to be sure the information on the map is correct, validating every rendition of your value stream map with the people who do the work is the best way to guarantee certainty that when the map is used for process redesign, it is a rock-solid base. Another approach is to have the workers involved in the process start the process by drawing from their memory and experience in a meeting by "walking" through the map and making adjustments as inaccuracies are recognized. Although this is sometimes easier and gets workers engaged from the beginning, be aware that it can create resistance if the initial contributors do not accept the changes that will occur with the upcoming future state map.

Using the Value Stream Map to Identify Problems With Flow

Even before hard data are added, the value stream map can be very useful to identify complexity, redundancy, and roadblocks in the flow of work (see Figure 5.2). Ideally all work would proceed with continuous flow. You would start the work, have all that you need on hand, be confident that each step of your work is safe and accurate, and have no interruptions occur. You would begin and finish the work with a clearly defined outcome in mind and know at the end that it was achieved.

This rarely happens in your busy workday and may never be completely attainable, but you want to constantly ask, "If that is ideal, how close can we get?" Defining the ideal state for each department, process, and activity is critically important for weighing decisions about the work. The information on the value stream map provides a foundation for that exercise.

When you scrutinize the CSM to understand flow, ask the following questions:

■ Is this process necessary? What is its purpose and could it be done a better way (or eliminated)? In our zeal to fix things, we sometimes jump into

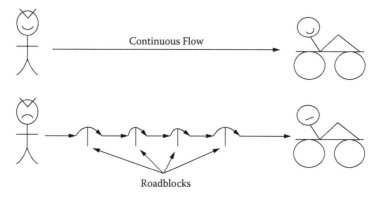

Figure 5.2

improving a process or a step that could be done away with or better accomplished another way. This first question allows you to truly evaluate the worth of the current condition. In the ever-changing environment of healthcare, it is easy to miss a transition or development that may make current practices obsolete.

■ Are all the steps in the process necessary? Are they adding value? Are they done consistently? Do they involve the fewest number of people? Are they generating and distributing complete information?

■ Are all the activities within the process boxes happening in the same order? Are they happening in the best order? Are there redundant activities in some steps that could be eliminated? Can some of the activities in one box be done better in another box? (In Figure 5.3, you can see the specific activities that occurred, and the order in which they occurred, to create the significant step called Admissions.)

■ Are the process boxes themselves in the best order? Is each one essential to the process? Can one or more be eliminated? Can they be combined and streamlined without sacrificing quality for the patient?

■ Is the information flow direct and simple? Is the information in each box original (not redundant) and can it be shared or eliminated?

■ If the current state map has more than four or five process boxes, is this complexity necessary? Can you complete the same work with fewer steps and fewer people without jeopardizing the quality to the customer?

Admissions
• Fill out history and physical form • Copy of insurance card • Sign HIPAA agreement • **Sign payment agreement**

Figure 5.3

Asking questions like these in order to deeply understand the work as it happens reveals unlimited opportunities to rearrange, eliminate, and enhance the activities of daily work. In Figure 5.4, you can review a current state map and ask these questions. Some of the problems identified by those questions are represented as storm clouds on the map.

Performance that parallels that of the Toyota Motor Company and other successful practitioners of lean can be achieved only by obtaining a deep understanding of the way work flows now and then methodically assessing each detail and activity within the work. The first view of the flow of work, illustrated on a simple but thorough value stream map of the current state, is a powerful step in making this happen. Discussion of information represented on a current state map should lead to one essential question: What about the way this work is happening now *is not* ideal? The dialogue that follows when you ask that question will lead to the inevitable suggestions for a better way to work and the design of a future state map for this process. The deep understanding realized from a current state map will act as the springboard for the creation of a future state map (see Chapter 6), which is a step toward reaching the ideal state.

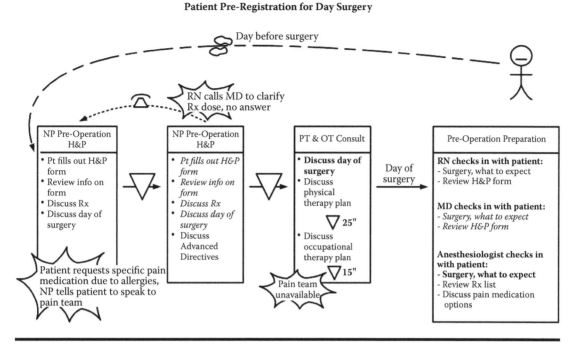

Figure 5.4

Adding Data to the Current State Map

Once the flow of a current process is understood, data can be added to the map that will measure time passing in each of the process boxes and deltas. Compiling data for the simple evaluation of best, worst, and average times in a process should not take long and will offer objectivity and credibility to the final assessment of the process.

Process engineering principles indicate that for process evaluation, 30 measurements should be adequate to establish statistical significance. You want to observe something 30 times before assigning an average number to it. However, if you imagine 30 measurements as a good number to give you a clear picture, then if the process occurs infrequently and all you want is a quick view, you may only need to measure 8 or 10 occurrences. Obviously if patient safety or dramatically changing people's behavior is at stake, you may need to collect more information than 30 samples. Do not get hung up on the numbers in data collection, just make it fit the objective of your investigation.

Knowing How to Collect Data

Timing activities on a current state map is not difficult if the process boxes are clearly and accurately defined and the deltas are placed correctly. As the process is timed, you will be gathering information related to when value-adding activities happen. For example, in Figure 5.5, notice that the first activity inside a

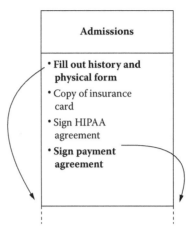

Figure 5.5

process box initiates the recording of time passing in that box, and the completion of the final activity in the box concludes the timing.

You will also be doing the math to understand the time that passes between those steps, which will be recorded on the map under the deltas. In the request process, for example, you can anticipate that travel, waiting, and information sitting in a mailbox are all not adding value and will have a delta drawn interrupting the line, as in Figure 5.6.

If you engage the people who actually do the work in this process of collecting data (as it relates to their part in the process), you gain a couple of advantages. If the staff records the start and stop times of pertinent steps in the process, no one needs to follow them around with a stopwatch. But be sure to make the staff comfortable with the process of measuring value in their work. If they feel threatened by this measurement activity, they are likely to fudge the data and skew the results. If you can alleviate their anxiety and they see the opportunity of recording actual time observations, doing this timing will lead to a heightened awareness of the steps in the process as well as ownership of the investigation that goes along with the work. When the people who are doing the work take the time to look at their activities with a spirit of ownership and improvement, great ideas surface that may otherwise go undiscovered.

For staff to successfully (and willingly) participate in the measurement of processes and wait times, the following must occur in advance:

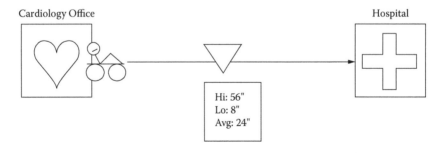

Figure 5.6

- The staff must be advised of why, when, and for how long the data collection will occur. (Thirty occurrences of many processes, like lab specimen collection or the admission of a new patient, can happen in a few hours or a few days.)
- Establish and indicate one unit of measure on the sheet (such as seconds, minutes, hours, or days) without mixing them. Even if the minutes climb into the hundreds or thousands for some activities, do not resort to converting them to a different measure. It will be much more difficult to compare times in the boxes, and eventually to improve those times, if a standard unit is not used for each project.
- Use a visual tool that reminds workers when and what to collect. Creating a tool, such as the example in Figure 5.7, on brightly colored paper that can be attached to a chart that flows with each patient puts no demands on the worker to remember to collect the requested information. If a visually unavoidable form passes through their hands in the course of their work, they are likely to take a few seconds to jot down the requested information. On the other hand, if a folder of data collection tools is placed in a forms drawer out of sight of the worker, it is easy to predict that compliance will fail.
- Create a designated drop-off at the end of the process to collect the finished data-collection tools. The easiest way to do this is to attach a blank version of the tool (another reason for it to be bright and visible) onto a large envelope that can be posted where the last person to fill in data can drop the finished form.
- Report the collected information back to the staff. They will be willing to participate only if they can see the value in their participation, and their sense of ownership in the process will increase as they are involved at every step. They are not collecting data for you, they are collecting data for the improvement of their work and will appreciate feedback from their contribution. Because you will be collating the information on a value stream map, it will be easy to read and understand, which means that even those who have little interest in statistics will recognize the significance of the numbers.

Data Collection Tool

		PT. Number __4__
Began Check-In	10 : 02	
Finished Check-In	10 : 08	
Began RN Consult	10 : 18	
Finished RN Consult	10 : 27	
Began MD Consult	11 : 11	
Finished MD Consult	11 : 24	
Began Check-Out	11 : 29	
Finished Check-Out	11 : 34	

Figure 5.7

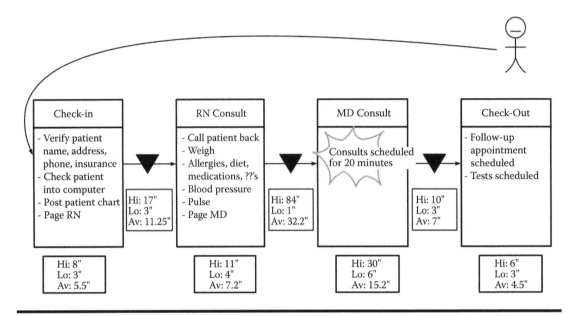

Figure 5.8

When creating a data collection tool, it is imperative that the initiating and concluding activities are agreed upon by the staff so that the timing information is consistently acquired. This means that first the flow and activities of the process boxes must be approved by the staff collecting the information and that the tool matches the steps. The example in Figure 5.8 illustrates this point.

Establishing Consistency

Be certain that the data collectors agree on the terms used to describe the work. Nothing is worse than collecting data and discovering that the words meant different things to different workers. The accuracy of the collected data will influence where you choose to focus your improvement efforts and is worthy of your early efforts.

Establishing data collection times is also important. If a process differs dramatically on the night shift compared to the day shift, confine the information gathered to a similar environment and create a value stream map for each shift. Likewise, similar work on one unit may differ on another unit. The very fact that similar work is not standardized may be part of your discovery, but the picture may be clouded if the different environments contribute to skewed data. Be sure to isolate time and space environments to ensure accuracy in your collected data.

Note: There should be a ***comments*** section on the data collection tool for staff to indicate if the process is purposefully being altered for any reason. Not completing the process or offering less value to achieve better times is not the object!

Existing data can be used only if it fits the in and out activities of the process boxes. Attempts to build a value stream map to fit existing data are almost always futile unless the data points match the boundaries of the process boxes. This almost never occurs unless a previous value stream map has been done to establish the data fields. In this consideration lies the possibility that previously collected data may have been less meaningful in its interpretation due to the struggle to have it make sense. When data are collected and reported on a well-drawn and collaborated value stream map, the information compiled is easy to read and understand. This motivates staff to consider the consequences of the way the work is happening now and to be open to redesigning old work habits. Do not be quick to disregard existing data that you may have on file, but evaluate it closely for its appropriateness on a current state map.

Evaluating the Numbers

Once the data collection is complete, the numbers can be collated and evaluated. Using basic math, significant information can be distilled by recognizing the lowest and highest numbers for each data set.

- **Lowest number:** The lowest number reflects the shortest amount of time required to complete the step being measured. You might consider this the best-case scenario, and this might become the number to which you aspire.
- **Highest number:** Conversely, the highest number collected illuminates the most time used for the activities in the box, highlighting an unusually complex set of activities or one in which many interruptions or work-arounds may have occurred.

Simple averaging of the times collected for each sample will give you a ballpark idea of the average time the activities in each of the process boxes requires.

There is no need to actively measure the time when nothing is happening between the boxes. Instead, the relevant numbers can be noted under the deltas after subtracting the start time for box 2 from the end time for box 1 and each subsequent delta the same way, as in Figure 5.9.

Again, the lowest number under the delta demonstrates the shortest delay between essential steps and the highest number points to the longest wait. This delay information is sometimes the first and biggest surprise when you start to evaluate work. It also points to one of the two greatest differences between value stream maps and flowcharts. Basic flowcharts generally map how a process is *intended* to happen and do not capture the time when *nothing* is happening. The deltas indicate when no value-added activities are occurring. Value stream maps illustrate the way (or many ways) the work is really happening now and highlight clearly when delays occur that prevent the work from moving forward. The measure of the delay enables you to determine how much of the total time spent in the process is value-added versus non-value-added to the patient or

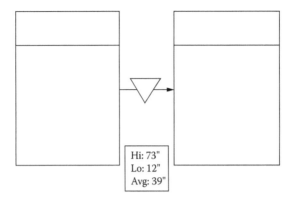

Figure 5.9

customer. From these numbers you can construct a value quotient that indicates the percent of waste in a process through the eyes of the customer.

Information collated and evaluated this way gives you an unbiased view of the most timely completion of any of the steps in the process, the lengthiest investment in the step, and a simple average of how much time is consumed in the sample studied. An example of data added to the map in this fashion is shown in Figure 5.10.

As an example, if the shortest time observed in one process box is 5 minutes, the longest is 7 minutes, and the average is 6.1 minutes, you would be less likely to focus on that box if another box had a greater variation, such as a low of 5 minutes, a high of 19 minutes, and an average of 13 minutes. This allows you to see, without opinion or conjecture, where you should explore more deeply and focus on specific problem solving.

In the case of the latter, you could ask the following questions to better understand the variance in the numbers:

■ Why can you sometimes complete these activities in 5 minutes?
■ What is it about the work that is going well in that situation that might be replicated?

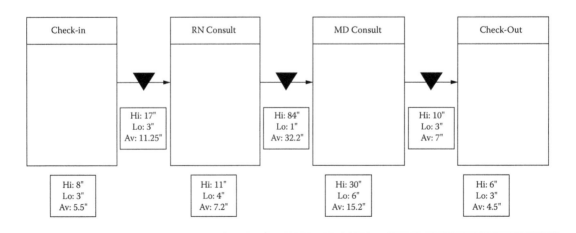

Figure 5.10

- What occurs to increase the time to 19 minutes in the longest recorded entry?
- What happened repeatedly to develop an average that keeps you from producing the best time, most of the time, as indicated by the average?

These questions can be answered only by going back to the worksite and observing more closely to obtain detailed information from the people who do the work.

Sometimes exceptional outlying circumstances occur that affect the numbers, and those should be considered for exclusion to not skew the picture. Common sense must prevail with the evaluation of simple data. However, if outliers repeatedly show up, you want to ask why there are so many outliers, and consider whether an upstream step might be creating a "consistent inconsistency" in the work.

Using data to analyze a process for weakness is key to success with value stream maps. Communicating observations in a nonthreatening spirit of improvement, but one that is scientific in nature, elicits insightful ideas for change that are supported by the source of the work—the people who accomplish it.

Reporting Your Discoveries

The power of presenting a good current state map with the following statement should not be underestimated: "This is the way the work is happening now. Is it good enough?" This is a provocative question that initiates deep thinking, using a base of solid data from which to launch ideas, that is infinitely more motivating than a statement of despair. Rather than stating the obvious, using the Socratic (questioning) method reveals significant process problems and generates individual awareness of flaws in work. It also takes the investigation to a new level by digging deeper into the problematic work by mining the knowledge locked in the experience of the worker. It is only when processes are examined at this level of detail that really innovative ideas for redesign and reducing waste can occur.

As you move on to the next step, creating a future state map (see Chapter 6), do not discard your current state map in your enthusiasm for fixing the work. There is much to be learned by reflecting on the original condition of the process, even when future iterations are undertaken. Over time, many iterations of one map may be done as conditions for that work change. This is a good thing! When you recall that Toyota has been practicing TPS for close to 70 years, it is clear that this way to work is really the practice of pragmatically examining work and adapting to changes.

The rigor required to deeply understand the current condition through observation, data collection, and deep analysis of the information—with the people who do the work—prepares you for the next step, developing a vision of a better way to work using a future state map.

Summary

Value stream mapping gives you a fresh and objective way to look at work. When you create your first map, begin with a process that is easy to observe and offers enough repetitive events to measure quickly. Your first current state map will open your eyes to the nature of work that can be understood, evaluated, corrected, and communicated with this simple pencil-and-paper method. Subsequent experience will enable you to add depth and more complex information to your map, but you will find that these simple building blocks and activities will remain at the foundation of all successful value stream maps.

Chapter 6

Building the Vision: The Future State Map

With the deep understanding attained while creating the current state map (CSM), you can now come up with a better way to work. You do have to hold yourself back; however, the tendency to run out and make changes when problems are recognized needs to be curtailed until the future state map (FSM) is created, and this is not always easy! A refreshing feature of creating a future state map and plan lies in the methodical consideration not only of the identified faults of the process, but also using the same consideration for the remedies.

Using the original current state map as a base may be an option for starting the future state exercise, or you may find that a completely new foundation may need to be drawn. The same rules apply, however: The future state map is laid out the same as a current state map and always starts with the person initiating the request. Each step is drawn and an indication of information flow is recorded, just like on the current state map. The difference with this map is the good ideas that arose from review of the current state map are included in the design of the process as you envision it occurring in the future. The map is, as with the current state map, drawn with a pencil and should use the same icons and units of measure as the initial document.

Defining "Future"

Defining the "future" involves some thought. It is easy to confuse the future state with ideal. Remember that ideal is the gold standard for perfection toward which you are always striving, but it may not be achievable in the current fiscal and technological state of your organization. A future state map must (1) be achievable and (2) move you *closer* to the ideal state. So it is a target state that is moving you ever closer to ideal, but it is not necessarily completely ideal yet. With every new design or change that is made on the FSM, the operative question is, "Will this change move the work closer to ideal?" Constantly reflecting on what was not ideal about the current state highlights the necessary changes to be built into the new process.

Being Realistic About the Future

Creating a map that reflects changes that can be realistically achieved on a defined timeline includes consideration of the following:

- You have the human resources to make the changes happen (people who can realistically make time to see the improvements through to completion).
- You have leadership support of the improvement. (Where does this work fall in the strategic plan of the organization or department? Who "owns" it on the administrative team?)
- You have a realistic date for experimenting with new ideas and reflecting on changes.
- You are realistic in your consideration of constraints, such as cost and other initiatives scheduled on the unit.

Creating the future state map is the next activity after the evaluation of the current state map and should reflect its layout features. The future state map will reside with the current state map, in a folder or binder, as a ready reference as improvement activities proceed. Better yet, install an inexpensive bulletin board in a prominent place on the work unit where the current maps can be seen and commented on by staff and management. In this way, as the new way to work is visualized on paper, it can be compared side-by-side with the current state map to confirm that old wasteful habits are not being carried onto the new design.

Designing the Future

As mentioned in Chapter 5, the first question to ask is whether this process is essential in the first place. If the process is antiquated or obsolete, do not put a lot of energy and resources into fixing it when you could eliminate it. Perhaps the future state map should reflect a completely new way to achieve the requested service.

Asking whether each step is necessary along the way should be repeated with every entry on the map. Reducing the number of ways that a request can be made is almost always key to reducing errors in the subsequent delivery of the request and is significant in lowering the frustration level for the people involved in both ends of the request. Figure 6.1 is a great example of a real value stream map that illustrates the many options and people that could be involved

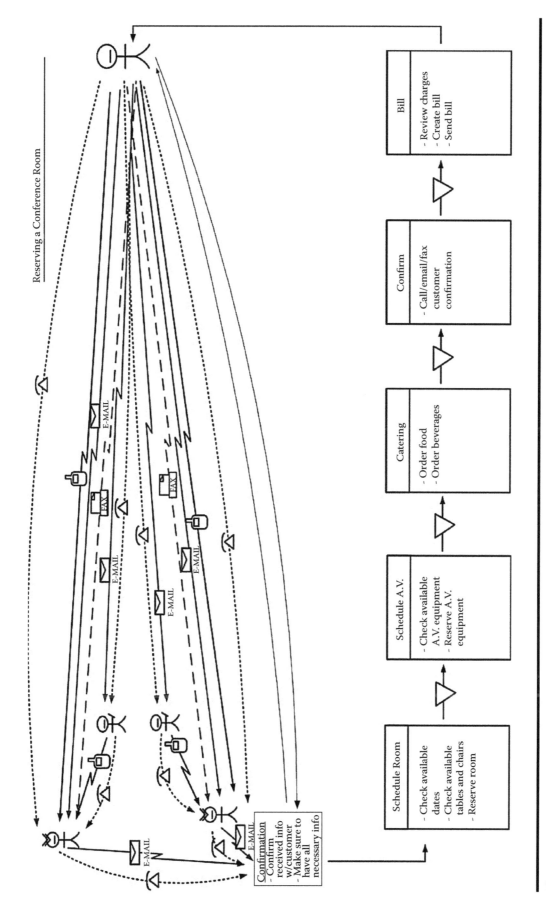

Figure 6.1

in requesting a meeting room reservation. It is easy to understand why variation and lack of clarity in making a request can generate confusion and introduce errors further downstream in the process.

Activities inside process boxes may need to be eliminated or combined, and the number of steps (process boxes) may be reduced or placed in a different order. The time spent in each process box may be redefined and a plan for how to eliminate non-value-added activities within it will be developed as the next step in cutting wasted activities.

Sometimes the steps in a process are necessary and in the right order, only the times to perform them are inconsistent. On the future state map, the staff can set a standard for how long each step should take, and the map will look different only if the times change in the data slots. These numbers are not assigned randomly! They are calculated from the real data that were collected on the original CSM and take into consideration how the work can be done when the obstacles have been removed. After the improvements have been made and a *new* current state map is created, the real data can be compared to the proposed numbers on the future state map to evaluate the accuracy of the projection. This valuable assessment of data is quick, logical, and can be clearly understood by all staff.

Once the improved request process is drawn on the future state map, compare it to the current state map and visually evaluate whether it looks cleaner, simpler, and more direct. If the answer is a resounding "yes," and all the necessary information is being conveyed, you have taken the first step in improving the process. If the complexity is not reduced or more steps are added, it is time to go back and observe the process to discover a way to eliminate the redundancy.

Almost always the first rendition of a future state map can be improved upon as the team more deeply understands the work. Do not be frustrated if the first iteration requires revision, because it most certainly will! This is a journey of continuous improvement, and the results will depend on the depth of discovery and willingness of the improvement team to expose problems.

Validating the future state map with the people who do the work is at least as important as it was in confirming the current state map. The staff that owns the process, who performs this work every day, will have ideas for doing it better than the most imaginative outsider could ever develop. Be sure to take the pencil-drawn future state map to the staff for validation and suggestions for even more improvement. The willingness of the author of the future state map to erase and redraw it based on staff input will produce immediate and lasting support for the proposed better way to work. For accuracy and buy-in to change, it is essential that the people who do the work are considered the resident experts and are actively involved in creating a better way to work.

Now that there has been deep understanding achieved by the current state map and ideas for a proposed better way to work visualized on the future state map, it is time to organize the improvements in the next step, the future state plan.

The Future State Plan: Planning A3 Problem Solving

Although the temptation is to run out and fix problems as soon as they are revealed, a well-thought-out plan for attending to all the details of the proposed improvements is a sound investment of resources. The future state plan builds accountability and sets realistic time goals for specific activities that will move the process from the current state to the predicted future state. Those activities will be chosen to remove the roadblocks that were identified on the initial current state map.

The plan will include the following:

- *What* needs to be done
- *How long* it will take to realistically be completed
- *Who* will take responsibility for each improvement
- The anticipated *outcome* for each activity

By defining what needs to happen, by whom, by when, and with what expected outcome, you very clearly and realistically specify the work for the problem solvers involved. This is your work list; it specifies the work and everyone involved knows exactly what is expected of them. See the example in Figure 6.2.

Each of the improvements in the plan will involve a number of people over a span of time. This must be considered seriously to create a realistic, achievable strategy. It is not acceptable to verbally assume responsibility to get things done without having the time and outcome clearly defined. We have all experienced the good intentions that are offered in conventional meetings and the disappointment and frustration generated by failed promises. Likewise we have been victims of unrealistic plans that are either unachievable or interfere with daily work commitments. Instead, expectations must be defined and deadlines set to assist the team in time management and a solid campaign for success. Without this clarity of commitment, busy workers are likely to forget or not schedule the necessary work that lies behind each of these rigorous assignments.

Administration needs to be apprised regularly of the improvements' progress and resource allocation. The solid documentation of the current and future state

What	Who	When	Outcome
1. Stock patient rooms	CJ	4/09	Resources at bedside
2. Standardize patient admission form	JO/SS	4/15	Same form used by all
3. 5S the storeroom	DW/JO	4/10	Storeroom easy to use
4. Create missing medication policy	SS/RX	5/1	Quick access to meds

Figure 6.2

maps and the plan of action for change provide a quick and visual format for keeping busy administrators engaged.

On a local level, providing a bulletin board or other wall space within a work unit to display active maps and plans is a good way to maintain staff awareness of improvements in motion. Be sure to report when a process sees significant change. Everyone appreciates knowing the results of their contribution, even if it is only validation.

The plan should be developed by the authors of the current and future state maps and the workers who will be participating in the improvements. Like the maps used to this point, the plan needs to be visual and displayed prominently in the work area and also distributed to the team. The plan must be easy to read and realistic to achieve.

As with the maps before it, the plan should be validated by the people doing the work to ensure its successful design. When the improvement team meets to report progress, the plan should be reviewed and altered as needed to include current changes in circumstances and new knowledge gained. Each action item in the plan should be evaluated for progress:

- Is it on time?
- If not on time, what delayed the progress and how should it be re-timed?
- Does it need to be scrapped?

This is not a test, it is a work in progress, and the simple but pragmatic use of pencil-drawn diagrams celebrates forward momentum and avoids confused interpretations of expectations, progress, and outcomes.

Understanding A3 Problem Solving

The work defined in the future state plan is usually done using A3 problem solving or another lean method. While the value stream map is used as a way to see and understand work from 10,000 feet, A3 problem solving uses the same logic but focuses on specific problems with the detail of a microscope. It is the accumulation of problems within the activities in the process boxes that causes the work to be unreliable and inconsistent. By addressing those specific obstructions using the A3 method, the overall performance of the mapped process will be improved, as is reflected in the data collected after the A3 improvements have been implemented. The same lean thinking is applied to both the value stream map and A3 problem solving, but on a different scale. Using both enables you to see the big picture of how a process flows (value stream mapping) and to zero in on the specific problems within it (A3 problem solving). In both views you are looking at

- How the work happens now

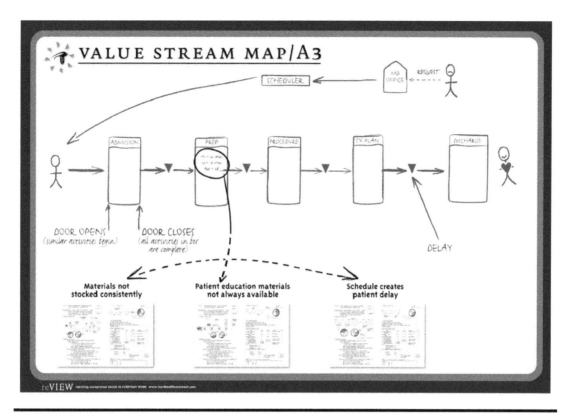

Figure 6.3

- What obstacles are in the way of the work happening with continuous flow
- What about the work is and is not ideal

This initial understanding is critical to developing a better way to work that is sound, reliable, and durable with the people who do the work. Figure 6.3 demonstrates the relationship between VSM and A3.

The Anatomy of an A3 Report

A3 problem solving is a method for structured problem solving created with a pencil on a piece of 11 inch × 17 inch paper. Outside the United States, this paper size is referred to as "A3," thus the name. An A3 report is a storyboard of sorts that visualizes how a process happens now, what is wrong with it, and why it happens the current way—all on the left side of the paper. The right side then illustrates a proposed better way to work, what needs to change, a plan for changing it, the cost:benefit ratio of the change, and tested proof that the change is a good idea. As specific problems are addressed with A3 problem solving, work processes will improve, as will be indicated by subsequent value stream maps of that process.

There may be many A3 opportunities recognized in one process box with significant variation in the data, or one significant obstacle may be creating problematic delays and interruptions. By following the basic premise that all work can only be improved when it is deeply understood, you can use VSM and A3 problem solving to not only achieve that understanding, but also to communicate it simply and quickly.

A3 problem solving, like VSM, is borrowed from the Toyota Motor Company and adapted to manufacturing in the United States and elsewhere, and has now been demonstrated to be of value in healthcare in every department that wants to reduce waste and errors and retain good employees. Data collected in the value stream map shows statistically (and thus objectively) where there is variation in each step and indicates opportunities to remove barriers around which the worker must work to produce the step. It is these workarounds and reworks that you attempt to remove with the A3 process in order to improve the value stream.

A3 problem solving is a way to look with "new eyes" at a specific problem identified by direct observation or experience specifically revealed from a completed value stream map. It offers a structure that begins by always defining the issue through the eyes of the customer, and this way of stating the problem makes resolution of the problem indisputable. After all, why are we all here if not to continuously improve the service or product for the customer or patient?

Objectivity is further reinforced by a deep understanding of the current condition before jumping to a solution. When you observe and draw the current condition that allowed a specific problem to occur, the method does not assign blame to anyone, but simply acknowledges that this is the way the work happens now, with or without flaws. Once that first view of the problem is seen, you can move on to ask, "What about the way this work is happening is not ideal?" The problems recognized within the current condition drawing are added to the graphic as "storm clouds." These are the problems that will be more deeply explored in the root cause analysis.

Getting to the Root Cause

Root cause analysis is not new to proess improvement, but A3 problem solving offers a simple and consistent way to achieve and record it. Toyota's *Five Why's* approach to getting to the root cause of problems identified as storm clouds is easy to remember and easy to execute. The process is simple: You continue to ask "why?" over and over (more than five times, if needed!), as each answer reveals more layers. When the final "why?" reveals the root cause, you have found what must be addressed to remove the storm cloud and move the process closer to ideal. The answer to the final "why?" in the analysis of each storm cloud/problem creates a checklist for what you need to do later in the implementation plan on the right side of the A3 document. As you work through the A3 problem-solving process, you can refer back to the root causes on the left side of the page and ask yourself, "Have we removed the causes that are keeping us from achieving the target condition?" A simple A3 problem-solving process is presented in Figure 6.4 to

ISSUE Medical record submitted to coding department without MD dictation after patient is discharged.

BACKGROUND

MDs work 12 hour shifts, work eight shifts/month.
RNs work 12 hour shifts.
Charge nurse on each shift.
Ward clerk from 6am until midnight.

Average accounts receivable days: 91
In one month there were 23 charts without MD dictation.

CURRENT CONDITION

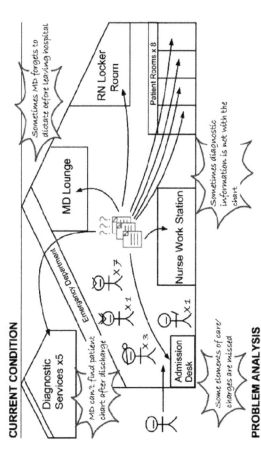

- MD can't find patient chart after discharge
- Sometimes MD forgets to dictate before leaving hospital
- Some elements of care/ charges are missed
- Sometimes diagnostic information is not with the chart

Diagnostic Services x5 — Emergency Department — Admission Desk — MD Lounge — RN Locker Room — Nurse Work Station — Patient Rooms x 8

PROBLEM ANALYSIS

1. Sometimes MD forgets to dictate before leaving hospital
   why? There are many charts to keep track of on a busy shift
   why? MD relies on memory
   why? No other system.
2. MD can't find patient chart after discharge
   why? Not clear if other staff member is using the chart
   why? No defined chart location
   why? Chart not where MD left it
   why? No assigned location for the patient chart
3. Sometimes diagnostic information is not with the chart
   why? Person responsible for compiling diagnostic information can't find the chart
   why? No assigned location for the chart when patient returns to ED
4. Some elements of care/charges are missed
   why? MD dictates on a patient that he hasn't seen for days
   why? Chart goes to coding before MD has dictated on it
   why? Not always clear if MD has dictated
   why? No chart completion indicator/checklist

TARGET CONDITION		Title: ED Chart Organization
		TO: Susan
		BY: Alicia
		DATE: September 1, 2006

All workers know where patient and chart are in the flow of care.

MD knows when chart is complete/ when patient is discharged

New Patient | RN Exam Complete | MD Orders | To Diagnostic Department | From Diagnostic Department | MD Discharge | RN Discharge

Nurse Work Station

COUNTERMEASURES

1. Create designated location for chart
2. Create a checklist for the front of the chart where each caregiver can acknowledge completion of steps of care.

IMPLEMENTATION PLAN

What	Who	When	Outcome
Order colored boxes	WC	9/5/06	Clear signal of chart location
Inform staff when boxes are installed	CN	9/16/06	Begin new process
Develop charting checklist	CN	9/10/06	Quick reference to completed charting

COST / BENEFIT

Cost		$$$
	Colored boxes	$35
	Staff time	$110
Benefit		$$$
	Reduce accounts receivable days	More $$
	Improve time to patient care	Quality

TEST

Spray paint cardboard boxes to use for chart steps. Coders evaluate charts for level of completion for one week. Evaluate for changes.

FOLLOW UP

January 10, 2007
Accounts receivable days reduced to 42 days.

Figure 6.4

help you understand the fine level of investigation that is required to identify each specific problem and how the *Five Why's* are used to get to the root cause.

Coming Up With Countermeasures

The right side of the page is the creative and fun half of the A3 report. Because you enter it with such a deep understanding of the current work (from the left side), and because you have done the root-cause work on the first half of the A3 report, a target condition is created that is also a sketch of how the improved work will look. When the drawing is complete, you can compare the target condition to the current condition and ask the essential question, "Does this new proposed way to work move us closer to ideal?" If the answer is yes, you can move forward to clearly defining countermeasures, those changes that you need to make in the process to move from the current to the target condition. The countermeasures will represent significant process adjustments and may require many specific tasks to be accomplished. Most A3 reports have between one and three vital countermeasures recognized to improve the work. As with the work done on the left side of the A3 report, the target condition and countermeasures need to be team activities, with ideas and validation from the affected parties that the suggested changes will indeed improve work flow and effectiveness.

Building accountability for the specific tasks that must be finished to accomplish the countermeasures is documented in the implementation plan. This implementation plan is essentially a work list, much like the future state plan, and includes the following information:

- What will happen with each numbered task
- Who will be responsible for its completion
- When it will be finished
- The expected *outcome*

The implementation plan ensures clarity in achieving the countermeasures' objective.

Administrative consideration for approval of the proposed change usually needs to include the cost of the implementation plan, as well as an estimate of the cost benefit. This information also offers motivation to make change happen (and stick!), because staff and managers can clearly measure the benefits against the investments of time and dollars required.

Because A3 problem solving is a rendition of the scientific method of problem solving, it requires a test that proves that the anticipated benefits can be realized with the suggested changes. The test may be done with a small sample of real events that are closely monitored or in a simulated environment, but either way, it gives staff and administration the confidence to move forward with implementation of the changes.

The last information recorded on the A3 report is follow-up. On each A3 report, the assignment of monitoring the effects of postimplementation changes is essential. The improvement team will determine (1) what will be monitored or measured, (2) who will do it, and (3) the frequency and dates of reporting. Follow-up is critical, because after implementation the follow-up information is the *new* current condition of how the work happens now. The team will evaluate that information and decide whether it is satisfactorily changed or whether there are even more opportunities to hone the work. New improvement efforts begin by moving the follow-up information to the current condition of a blank A3 report and progressing with the A3 method, thus creating the perfect iterative process for problem solving.

This brief overview of A3 problem solving is intended to provide you with a high-level understanding of how value stream maps and A3 reports work together. More instruction and several actual A3 case studies can be found in *A3 Problem Solving for Healthcare* (Productivity Press, 2008).

The *New* Current State Map: Closing the Loop

As discussed above, on each A3 report completed from the future state plan, follow-up information is collected on the assigned date(s). This gives the improvement team the opportunity to reflect on the results of their actions and decide whether the specific process needs another iteration of an A3 report to fine-tune remaining problems or if it is acceptable as completed. The same goes for value stream mapping.

Now that you have completed a current state map, a future state map, a future state plan, and all the A3 improvements assigned within it, it is time to measure again and see how you have done. This is going to look quite a bit like the future state map, but will reflect the reality of how that future state map is being implemented. How effective were your orchestrated changes? By this time, the individual or team that created the first current state map is so familiar with the process being evaluated that it does not take long to create a new current state map with new data to confirm how the work is flowing *now*. How are you delivering your service now that time, effort, and new work behaviors have been have invested? This new map will offer clear markers of change when compared against data on the initial current state map.

There may be new and detailed A3 problem-solving opportunities recognized on the new map. It is very interesting to put the original current state map and the new current state map that you have drawn side by side and look for the following elements:

- Is the new map easier to read?
- Are there fewer lines of communication in the request?
- Are there fewer steps (process boxes) in the delivery of the request?

- Are there fewer loops in the work?
- Are there fewer redundant activities within the process boxes?
- Are there fewer handoffs between providers?
- Are the delays between steps shorter?
- Are the times more consistent in each box? In other words, is there less variation?
- Do the changes correlate to other measures, such as patient and worker satisfaction surveys, improved patient throughput, and so on?

From these questions and many more, a decision can be made to happily accept the improved process as revised or to continue with another iteration, moving to a new future state map, new future state plan, and so on, always moving closer to ideal.

Summary

Of all the lean philosophies and practices that I have learned from manufacturers and students of Toyota who have been my mentors, by far the two methods that embody the concepts and strategies at the core of Toyota's renown are value stream mapping and A3 problem solving. They are much more than tools, although they are commonly included in what's known as "the lean toolbox." As these two simple methods and documents are understood and practiced together, they create a new way to think, not just at work, but in the activities of daily life as well.

Chapter 7

Sharing and Archiving VSMs Electronically

As previous chapters have shown, a paper-and-pencil approach is essential to drawing value stream maps. This approach can be complemented by transferring paper maps to electronic models for clarity, ease of sharing, archiving, and ease of calculation. I am grateful to Dilesh Patel for the contribution of this chapter's information about using a software tool (eVSM) designed for this purpose.

Electronic Value Stream Mapping (eVSM)

eVSM is a software tool designed to support maps and other visuals commonly leveraged in lean implementations, including value stream maps. Figure 7.1

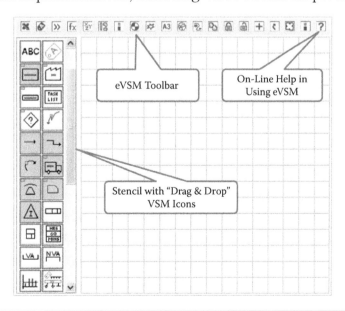

Figure 7.1

shows the working window of eVSM, with the drag-and-drop icons on the left. Figure 7.2 shows how eVSM can be used to create, analyze, and share a map. The map is drawn by dragging and dropping icons from the eVSM stencil.

eVSM Operation Icons

Let us review the main icons to be used. You simply drag and drop icons onto the page, then double-click the shape on the page to edit the text.

■ **eVSM arrow icons:** Straight, stepped, and curvable arrows are available (see Figure 7.3). Blue icons in the stencil have associated families of arrows that change in style and color. You simply right mouse click to access members of the family. Arrow ends glue to operation shapes and then move with them. Use of glue makes modifications much easier in the software. Curvable arrows have center control points that make it easy to shape them.

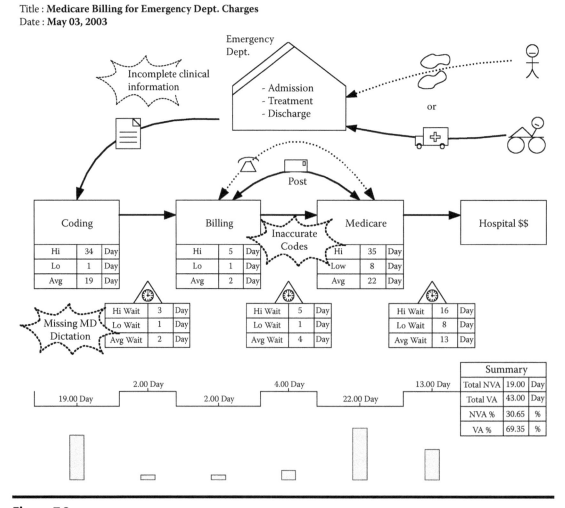

Figure 7.2

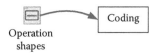

Operation
shapes

Figure 7.3

Figures 7.4 through 7.10 are examples of using curvable arrows to connect icons to and around other process boxes and icons in value stream maps. These arrows can be colored differently so that the flow of information, materials, and people can be effectively communicated on the same map without confusion. Another method of differentiating flows is using dotted, dashed, or solid arrows to connect a pathway.

■ **eVSM transport and transmit icons:** The transport icon in the stencil represents a family of icons for physical transport, such as an ambulance, gurney, or helicopter. The transmit icon in the stencil represents a family of icons for information transmittal, such as phone, e-mail, and fax. Transport and transmit icons can be glued to the underlying arrow so that they move automatically with the arrow. See Figure 7.5 for an example.

■ **eVSM delay icons:** eVSM has a family of icons (see Figure 7.6) representing delay due to wait times, in-boxes, and queues. Right mouse click on the shape to access other family members.

■ **eVSM data icons:** The map has timing data for activities and for waits, as shown in Figure 7.7. Numeric data are put on the map with eVSM data icons called name value units (NVUs).

■ **eVSM value-added (VA) and non-value-added (NVA) icons:** VA and NVA icons typically form a timeline at the bottom of the map and values on the timeline are calculated based on data collected on the map. Figure 7.8 illustrates a segment of a timeline in development.

■ **eVSM people icons:** eVSM people icons are deliberately simple so that they can be drawn by hand in the initial VSM activities. The person's expression can be set to happy, neutral, or unhappy. Shaded icons in the stencil represent an icon family. Members can be accessed with a right mouse click on

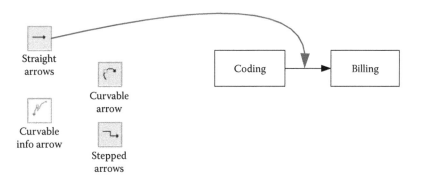

Figure 7.4

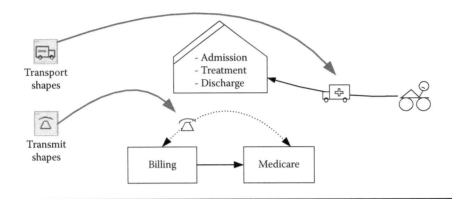

Figure 7.5

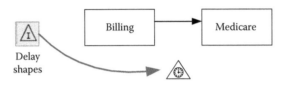

Figure 7.6

the shape. See Figure 7.9, which shows the power of including emotions on your drawing.

■ **eVSM callouts:** eVSM callouts are used to annotate the value stream map and can have additional properties added to them (such as owner, priority, and so on). An Excel report can be generated summarizing properties for each callout. The storm clouds and fluffy clouds used in A3 problem solving to indicate bad and good features, respectively, in callouts are illustrated in Figure 7.10.

eA3: A3 Reports for Problem Solving

The callouts and associated Excel report are often used to initiate improvement projects at the frontline level. A3 reports are then created for each improvement project. eA3 is an integrated function within eVSM developed to use similar icons

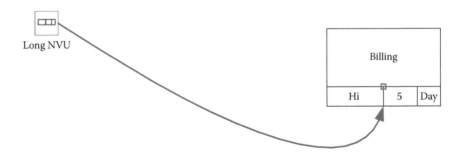

Figure 7.7

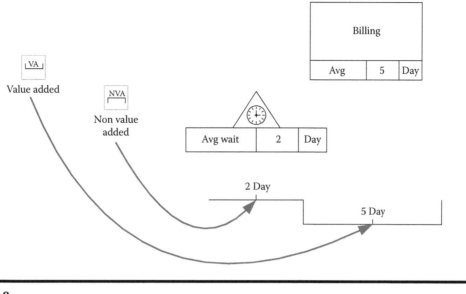

Figure 7.8

Figure 7.9

and methods to illustrate problem-solving efforts using an A3 report. eVSM and its integrated eA3 function require underlying Microsoft Office tools (Visio and Excel).

eVSM Equations

The Medicare billing value stream map has some raw data (such as average wait time), along with some calculated data (such as total VA time). Most of the calculations are trivial and can be done easily by hand. If so, the answers can be entered directly on the map, as was done with the raw data.

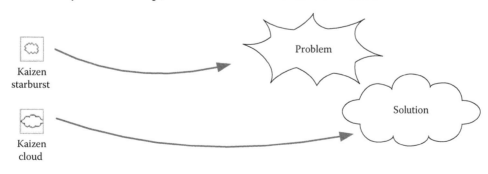

Figure 7.10

As maps get bigger and more complex, however, or are modified for what-if studies, these same calculations can get tedious. In some cases, it is worth writing some simple equations to automate the calculations. Let us look at the equations involved here, starting with the two timeline equations for the VA and NVA shapes in Figure 7.11.

Eqn 1: Value Added = Avg
Eqn 2: Non Value Added = Avg Wait

Now let us look at the four summary equations in Figure 7.12.

Eqn 3: Total VA = Sum (Value Added)
Eqn 4: Total NVA = Sum (Non Value Added)
Eqn 5: VA % = 100 * Total VA/(Total VA + Total NVA)
Eqn 6: NVA % = 100 * Total NVA/(Total VA + Total NVA)

eVSM has an equation manager where these six equations can be entered. They get automatically applied wherever the referenced variables exist. So if a

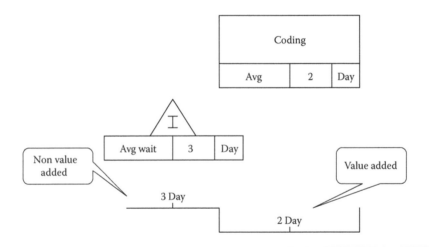

Figure 7.11

Summary		
Total NVA	19	Day
Total VA	43	Day
VA %	69.4	%
NVA%	30.6	%

Figure 7.12

new activity is inserted, no additional equations need to be written or modified. This makes for easy modifications.

eVSM actually processes the equations using an integrated Excel spreadsheet. This spreadsheet has a row for each tag (such as A010) and a column for each variable (such as Avg CT). The spreadsheet for the Medicare billing VSM is shown in Figure 7.13. You also have the option of writing equations in the spreadsheet directly if you are familiar with Excel.

eVSM Visual Gadgets

A primary purpose of a value stream map is to help visualize a process of work and where waste occurs so that improvement projects can be targeted. To make it easier to see the magnitudes of numbers on the map, you can optionally connect gadgets (like bars) to the numeric values. In the example in Figure 7.14, the bar height is scaled to the numeric values on the timeline, and in the completed map in Figure 7.15, the total information is compiled, with the quick-glance bars indicating the relationships within the process boxes and delays.

Tag	Operation	INV	INV	INV	VA	NVA	Data	Data	Data	Data	Data	Data	Data
		avg wait	hi wait	lo wait	value added	non value added	avg ct	hi ct	lo ct	nva %	total nva	total va	va %
		day	day	day	day	day	day	day	day	%	day	day	%
A010	Coding			34.00		19.00	34.00	1.00					
A020	Billing	2.00	3.00	1.00	5.00	3.00	2.00	5.00	1.00				
A030	Medicare	4.00	5.00	1.00	35.00	5.00	22.00	35.00	8.00				
A040	Hospital $$	13.00	16.00	8.00		16.00							
S010	Summary									30.65	43.00	24.00	69.35

Figure 7.13

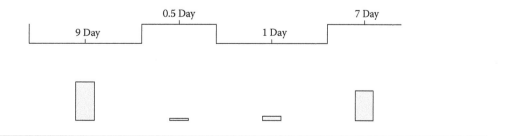

Figure 7.14

Title: **Medicare Billing for Emergency Dept. Charges**
Date: **May 03, 2003**

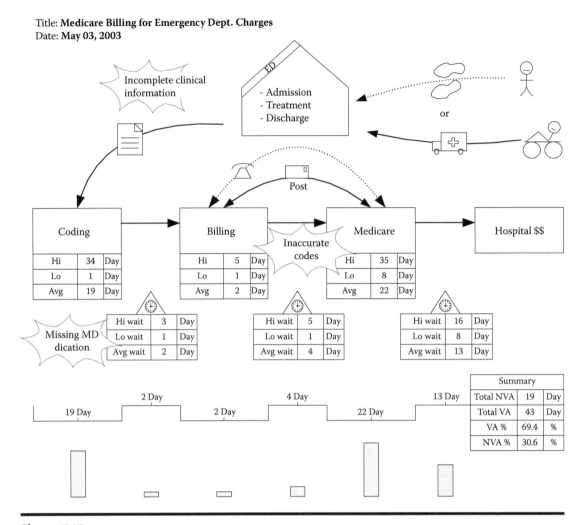

Figure 7.15

Summary

This chapter exposed the potential of expanding simple value stream mapping skills to include sophisticated data analysis and map design to provide a deep understanding of complex work. When communication of the mapped work is clean, articulate, and scientific, discoveries of improvements come quickly and from all levels of the workforce. Archiving and periodically reviewing previously completed maps also creates an opportunity to look at historical work with fresh eyes and experience. In fact, new opportunities may be missed without the diligent recording of work done by improvement teams; tools such as eVSM avoid gaps created by lost knowledge.

Chapter 8

Beyond the Simple Value Stream Map: Adding More Information

A basic value stream map has timing data and a summary box that totals the VA and NVA times. But there are several other variables that can help with the waste reduction goals of a lean implementation and that can be presented as numbers or visually on the map. Let us consider how these wastes are represented on the value stream map.

- **Waste—waiting for people or information:** eVSM represents a waiting room with a clock, as shown in Figure 8.1. Waiting for information to be processed is represented as an in-box.
- **Waste—measuring motion waste:** eVSM has a spaghetti diagram tool that lets you trace the movement of people on a floor plan and measure the approximate distance traveled. If the layout is poor or items are hard to find, the total distance traveled will be excessive. A sample spaghetti diagram drawn in eVSM with its associated report is shown in Figure 8.2 and clearly displays the travel problem. Transport or motion distances, once estimated, can be represented on the map under the transport or people icons, as in Figure 8.3.
- **Waste—excessive interaction/iterations:** A process can sometimes take an excessive amount of interaction, making it fragile because delay in one or more of the interactions can put the whole process at risk. You can build a

Figure 8.1

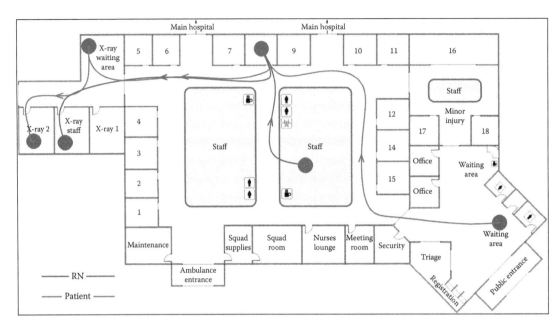

From	To	Color	Description	Date	Time	Distance	Duration	Type	Pathway
Waiting area	Bay 8					30			
Bay 8	X-ray waiting area					24			
X-ray waiting area	X-ray 2					15			
Main ER staff area	Bay 8					15			
Bay 8	X-ray staff room					29			
X-ray staff room	Bay 8					30			

Figure 8.2

from/to list like the one in Figure 8.4, and eVSM automatically creates a corresponding communications circle. The circle allows communication arcs to be highlighted and discussed. An improved process typically has fewer arcs, as shown in Figure 8.5. The number of "communications" or "handoffs" can be recorded on a high-level value stream map against each activity. A large number would merit detailed study. Suppose, for example, that an activity needed 10 communications and each communication was correct and timely 99% of the time. The overall activity would then be correct and timely about 90% of the time (99% multiplied 10 times).

■ **Waste—inventory:** Supplies in excess of requirements take up additional space, can become out of date, and (if distributed in multiple places) can create the need to "hunt" for an item. The inventory is represented on a map

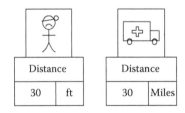

Figure 8.3

From	To
Patient	ER nurse
ER nurse	Floor nurse
Patient	ER nurse
Doctor	ER nurse
Doctor	Patient
ER nurse	Lab
Floor nurse	Service
Unit clerk	Transport
Doctor	ER nurse

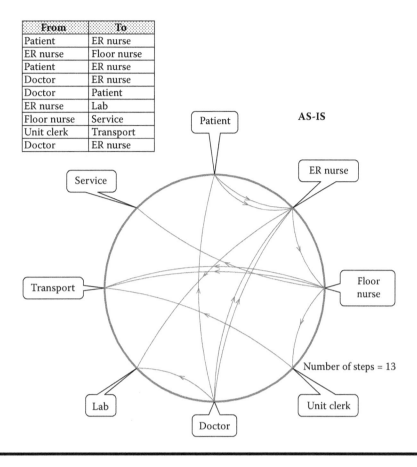

Figure 8.4

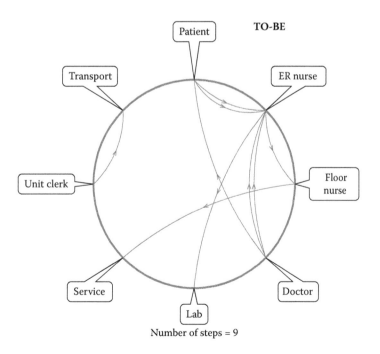

Figure 8.5

using an inventory triangle. It typically has a time calculation underneath it to show what length of time that inventory represents in normal usage. If the length of time is excessive, the inventory should be reduced. An example of how this would be indicated on the map is shown in Figure 8.6.

- **Waste—duplicate data entry:** Duplicate data entry not only increases work, but also introduces inconsistency errors that lead to further work. Whenever it is found, a kaizen burst (storm cloud) can be put on the map in the appropriate area; removal of the duplicate data should then be a candidate for an improvement project.

- **Waste—bottleneck processes lead to resource wastage:** A process that has a bottleneck effectively causes valuable resources to be wasted or idle in the remainder of the process. eVSM has bar charting capability to draw cycle-time charts to show where resources are over- and underutilized. In Figure 8.7, the "Take Sample" process takes longer than the target "Time Per Patient."

- **Waste—incorrect or incomplete data that causes rework:** One of the clearest examples of waste is one that occurs because of incorrect or incomplete data. In Figure 8.8, I added a variable called "Correct and Complete" to each activity. This measures the percent of time an activity was executed correctly the first time because all the incoming data was complete and correct. Note the cumulative effect of the "Complete and Correct" metric on the "First Time Quality" of the overall process. This measures how often a patient went through the whole process correctly the first time. The calculation for "First Time Quality" involves a multiplication of the "Complete and Correct" percentages of the activities.

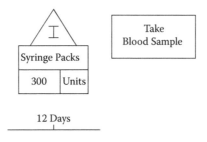

Figure 8.6

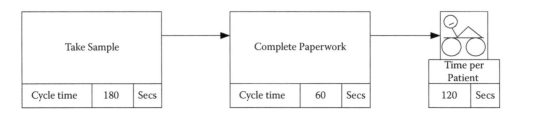

Figure 8.7

Title : **Medicare Billing for Emergency Dept. Charges**
Date : **May 03, 2003**

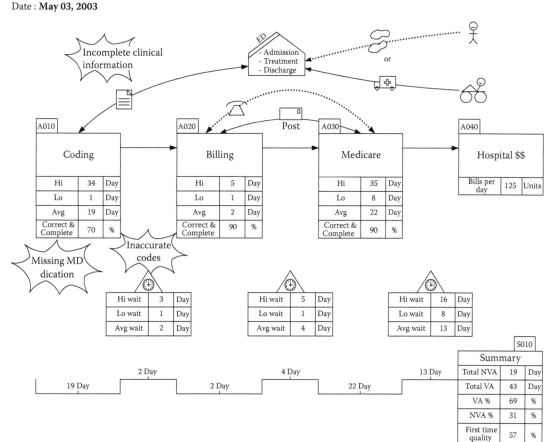

Figure 8.8

- **Waste—overprocessing and unnecessary activities:** I have already spoken about the impact of data duplication, mistakes, and incorrect or incomplete information. A lot of this can be seen at an individual activity level. When working within traditional departments, there can also be whole activities that seem necessary when looking just inside the department, but are unnecessary when seen together with activities in other departments. Often a department is also working to create data that an adjacent

Figure 8.9

St. Elsewhere Hospital
Current State Value Stream for Emergency Room
7-Mar-2007
HR/DP

Days	Shifts	Hrs
3	8	60
Shifts	Hrs	Mins

Summary

Total patients per day	75	Pts
Total admin time	45	Mins
Total RN time	80	Mins
Total MD time	40	Mins
Admin FTE	7.0	Staff
MD FTE	6.3	Staff
RN FTE	12.5	Staff

Registration

• Enter in DB
• Verify insurance

Admin time	15	Mins
MD time	0	Mins
RN time	0	Mins

Triage

• Check vitals
• Medical questionnaire
• Evaluation
• Complete form

Admin time	5	Mins
MD time	0	Mins
RN time	12	Mins

Emergency Room

• Re-check vitals
• Assessment
• Medical orders

Admin time	0	Mins
MD time	8	Mins
RN time	20	Mins

Radiology

• Prepare patient
• X-ray
• Radiology report

Admin time	5	Mins
MD time	12	Mins
RN time	8	Mins

Dx and Rx

• Diagnosis
• Treatment

Admin time	5	Mins
MD time	5	Mins
RN time	20	Mins

Discharge

• Report
• Patient instructions
• Return appointment
• Escort

Admin time	15	Mins
MD time	5	Mins
RN time	20	Mins

ED Staff

Summary

Total Pathway Time	210	Mins
Total VA time	105	Mins
Total NVA time	105	Mins
VA %	50	%
NVA %	50	%

Wait time	5	Mins

Registration

Process time	12	Mins

Wait time	5	Mins

Triage

Process time	14	Mins

Wait time	15	Mins

Emergency Room

Process time	22	Mins

Wait time	45	Mins

Radiology

Process time	12	Mins

Wait time	5	Mins

Dx and Rx

Process time	30	Mins

Wait time	30	Mins

Discharge

Process time	15	Mins

Patient

5.00 Mins / 12.00 Mins / 5.00 Mins / 14.00 Mins / 15.00 Mins / 22.00 Mins / 45.00 Mins / 12.00 Mins / 5.00 Mins / 30.00 Mins / 30.00 Mins / 15.00 Mins

Figure 8.10

department no longer uses. There are several approaches to tackling this problem with a value stream map. The first is to model the whole process on a single page as it weaves its way through multiple departments. eVSM has a swim-lane capability where each lane can represent a department. You can also color code activities by the department responsible. If the map becomes too complex, it is less effective as a visual tool, so you may find it useful to have multiple drill-down maps, where high-level maps have activities that are exploded on lower-level maps. On high-level maps it is useful to have an activity list inside the process boxes, as in Figure 8.9.

■ **Waste—from the provider or patient perspective:** Waste is often seen differently from the provider or patient perspective. For example, a hospital might be happy to maintain a queue of five patients in a room because of the chance that the hospital staff or equipment might have earlier availability. In this way, the hospital's resources would be maximized. From a patient's perspective, they might wait an average of 45 minutes longer than required. My book *Lean Consumption* describes this dual value stream between consumers and providers and suggests that the problem should be mapped by showing one value stream underneath the other and using arrows to show interaction between the two. This is easy to do in eVSM, and an example is shown in Figure 8.10.

CASE STUDIES

II

Case Study 1

Scheduling Meeting Rooms

Although scheduling meeting rooms may not at first blush appear to be significant in the operation of an acute care hospital, the reality is that many healthcare organizations have had to tackle this same process, because of frustration, confusion, and the waste of administrative, clinical, and staff time. I have chosen to include this map in order to clearly illustrate the complexity of the request process, which is commonly overlooked in traditional process improvement. I hope this exposure to the importance of understanding and simplifying the request step will inspire you to always scrutinize this important part of any process as carefully as the steps in the delivery of that requested service.

In this case, one of three of the education department staff responsible for booking conference rooms chose to examine this process after many complaints of double-booked rooms, rooms not prepared as requested for meetings and classes, and inaccurate assignment and directions to scheduled events. Caterers commonly arrived in the wrong locations, and the start of many meetings and classes was delayed as people scrambled to rectify the problems stated above.

The work on this value stream map was led by one individual, so no team was convened and no formal meetings were held to design a better way to work. However, the other room schedulers were involved in validating the map and contributing ideas for process improvement, and when a Web-based system was recommended using existing technology, a representative from the information technology (IT) department participated in facilitating the fix. Four "customers" from the administrative suite, the middle management staff, and the education department agreed to trial the three renditions tested before a final improved method was accepted and implemented.

File data were reviewed to understand the number of room reservations and cancellations made each month. I cannot overemphasize the power of understanding the magnitude of people and time affected by the inconsistent process! As in many daily examples, because this work was not "billable" or directly related to patient care and safety, it had never been considered for process improvement, despite the problems it caused for all meeting/class attendees and the staggering cost of these problems.

The astounding and obvious message portrayed in the first drawing of the current state (see Figure CS1.1) was that the request process was not clearly defined to the requestors, and many different methods (each with one or more unique opportunities to fail) were being used to communicate the request for a meeting space.

Actually booking, confirming, and communicating the arrangements thereafter were defined and consistent; in fact, in the redesign of the process, these steps were automated because they were documented to work well. The major changes were done upstream, early in the request process. Once those steps were standardized and communicated in the future state map (see Figure CS1.2), the downstream work occurred faster and more reliably.

As the IT department and the room scheduler looked at options for online reservations, their goal was to design a process that was error-proof, one that would not allow a requestor to make a request that could not be delivered. They created an online form that contained required fields that had to be completed, with seating and room feature limitations built into the form. The requests appeared in one color when the request was made on a shared electronic calendar and appeared in a different color when the reservation was

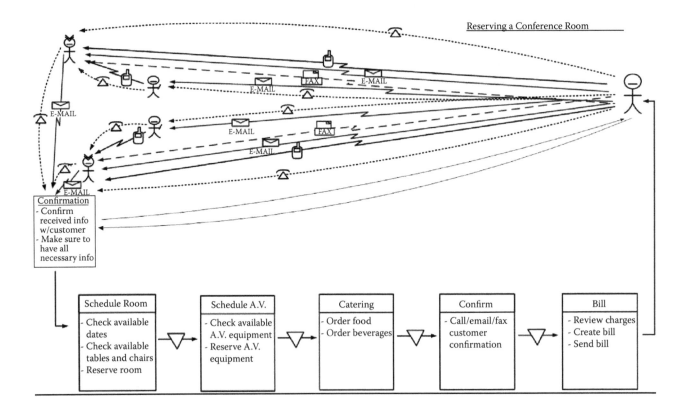

Figure CS.1

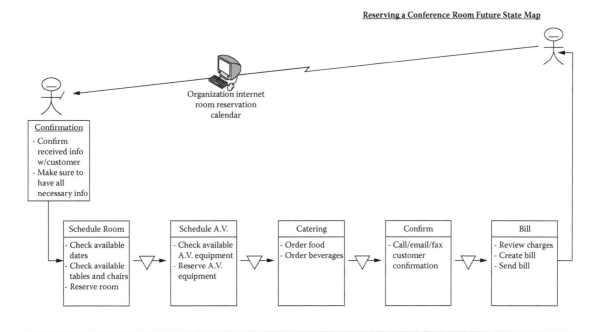

Figure CS.2

confirmed. This eliminated double booking, defined important requirements for specific types of meetings, and confirmed with the requestor the availability and location of the space he or she had requested. The room schedulers and caterers were able to view the current schedule in real time. Ten percent of the requests were recognized as "complex" and were handled in person by the reservations staff, but 90% of the daily requests were accommodated with the final process. With additional corrections to the process, automatic notification of meeting attendees was added to the system and clear directions to the meeting space were included.

It was recognized on the third rendition that meetings were scheduled back to back (which sometimes created problems if meetings went over the allotted time by a few minutes), and it was agreed hospital-wide that all meetings would be scheduled in increments of 20 or 50 minutes, with 10 minutes of "travel time" allowed between bookings.

As the new scheduling system was used by management and staff, many lively discussions about meeting effectiveness occurred. Questions arose such as

■ Why are most meetings scheduled for an hour?
■ Why are there so many agenda items on one meeting schedule?
■ How many meetings that I attend really pertain to my work?
■ Could we conduct fewer or more effective meetings?
■ Is the cost of our meeting time always justifiable?

An unexpected outcome of this work was the development of the meeting evaluation form in Figure CS1.3, which was created by the staff who did the initial value stream map and this author, and is now used by many organizations.

MEETING EVALUATION

Name and purpose of meeting:_____

Time planned for meeting:_____Actual time in meeting_____

Participants: Clerical_____RN_____Manager_____Technician_____MD_____

Administrator_____Other_____

Number of minutes relevant to me/my work: (Tic marks)_____

From the current agenda, could you create an activity design?

Activity   Time→* * 15* * 30* * 45* * 60* * 75* * 90* * 105* * 120

1._____

2._____

3._____

4._____

5._____

6._____

Could you create an implementation plan from the meeting discussion?

What	Who	When	Outcome

Reflection:

1. How much of the meeting added value to my work? (review tic marks)_____

2. What was the approximate labor cost of the meeting?_____

3. Did the value of the meeting justify the cost?_____My participation?_____

4. Was the agenda realistic?_____Was the time allowed adequate?_____

5. Did the participants leave understanding the implementation plan?_____

6. Could the work have been done better by small focus groups (2 or 3 people)?_____

Figure CS1.3

As a result of evaluating meetings around the organization, the following guidelines on conducting a lean meeting were created to maximize the value of meetings (based on the thinking and method used for A3 problem solving).

Ahead of time, prepare the members (as few as possible to represent the parties involved with the issue) that you will be using a new approach and focus primarily on one topic; be sure there is a whiteboard or flipchart and pens for drawing. Using principles of lean healthcare, the meeting leader would conduct a meeting with the following format:

1. Identify a meeting leader (one who understands lean thinking).
2. Introduce members (representing the parties affected by the process/problem).
3. Define the process of a lean meeting and proceed.
    - Define a single issue on which to focus at one time.
    - Assign the responsibility of drawing on the board to one member.
    - Have one member draw a paper copy as you progress.

The lean meeting leader, along with the group, will

1. Establish how the work happens now (have the assigned person draw on the whiteboard).
2. Determine the problems (go around the table and have each of the affected parties include his or her concerns) and add where they occur on the drawing as storm clouds.
3. Analyze those problems to determine the root cause as the Five Whys.
4. Determine and draw a target condition on which each affected party agrees.
5. Agree on countermeasures.
6. Create a realistic implementation plan to assign accountability for tasks.
    - What is going to happen?
    - Who will do it?
    - When will it be complete?
    - What is the expected outcome of each task?
7. Establish a date, time, and place to reconvene and report the results of the implementation plan.
8. Design a test of the plan.
9. Get approval of the implementation plan and test it.
10. Use the current condition, target condition, implementation plan, and test as minutes of the meeting and distribute them.
11. Conduct the test.
12. Meet again and report the results to the group; accept or redesign.
13. If satisfied, implement.
14. Schedule and conduct a follow-up review.

Case Study 2

Employee Continuing Education Tuition Reimbursement

It is never difficult to get staff to work on a process that will accelerate cash flow in their direction! This improvement initiative was done by a representative from human resources (HR), the education department, and a nurse from a clinical care unit. As their work progressed, they also engaged an information technologist.

The work was originated by the HR department which had been interrupted and frustrated by staff calls and e-mail inquiries related to education approval and tuition reimbursement. They were eager to satisfy the staff and remove the workarounds identified from their daily work. This improvement was quickly implemented, with pleasing results for all the affected parties.

Collection of new data was not required for the current state value stream map, as the documents currently used were all dated and the file information gave the team the information they needed to complete the map quickly. When the future state map was tested, matching data points were collected to verify the improved turnaround times.

The current state map was drawn first by simulating a typical request for approval of education support. The first obvious problem resided in the request process; there were four ways that a request could be submitted, each with inherent weaknesses. The staff was never quite certain which method would be fastest or most reliable, and some submitted multiple requests for fear of not using the system correctly. Obtaining a current request form was not always easy, as it could be obtained from HR, education, administration, or any of the unit directors or managers. Unfortunately not all those sources had updated forms, which meant that, sometimes, essential information was missing at the time of submission because an obsolete form was used.

The team first reviewed the different versions of the form that they gathered from various locations and recognized that there were six forms with the same title that listed different requirements and different directions for routing the form through the approval and reimbursement process. The multiple forms were consolidated and simplified. The new form eliminated two approval points (thus there were two fewer people to interrupt and two fewer opportunities to delay the process).

When the new form was agreed on by all parties, it was tested first by simulation. The information from an existing request was transferred to the new form, and it passed through the current process without question. The team then designed the future state map, in which the simpler form could be accessed through the hospital intranet, completed online, and submitted through the same system. Response to the requestor was rapid and reliable.

In a later iteration, parameters for approval were built into the system so that requests for standard courses under a prescribed dollar figure would not require human intervention. As employee records were converted from paper to electronic, use of their continuing education allotments became one of the electronic criteria for approval/denial, and even fewer requests required human processing. Those requests that fell out of the category were automatically forwarded to the HR department. An estimated 85% of requests were anticipated to be handled electronically, and reimbursement time for tuition decreased from 36 days to 3 days. Refer to and compare Figures CS2.1 and CS2.2 to see the measured improvement of this work.

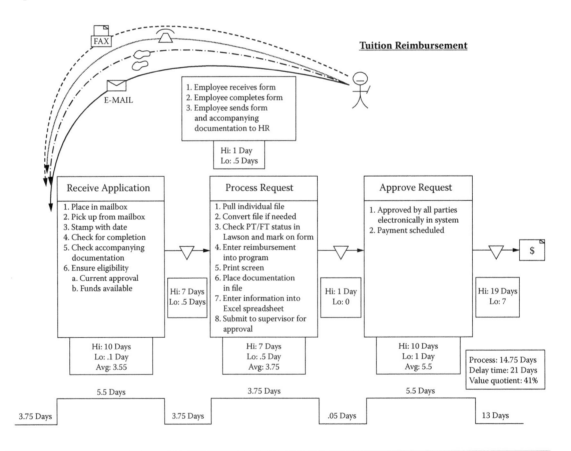

Figure CS2.1

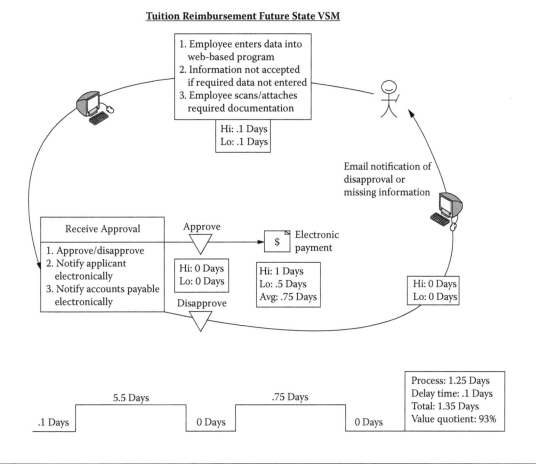

Tuition Reimbursement Future State VSM

Figure CS2.2

Case Study 3

Routine Medication Ordering (Physician Order)

Medication ordering is one of the most common activities in any acute or long-term care facility that serves inpatients. With a traditional paper chart system, a physician evaluates a patient's current status and writes an order on a paper chart that is transcribed by a clerk, checked by a nurse, and ordered from an in-house or local community pharmacy. The medication is then delivered to the work unit and ultimately administered by a nurse to the patient. Although many hospitals are moving toward electronic order entry, which may reduce the number of steps in this process, at the time of this writing more than two-thirds of acute and long-term care facilities in the United States still use paper for this important work.

This particular lean initiative took place in the rehabilitation unit of an acute care hospital. Concerns of physicians, nurses, and the unit clerks were voiced repeatedly regarding delays in the administration of medications, errors in transcription, omission of new medications to the medication administration record (MAR), and illegibility of the written orders. By their own admission, many previous attempts had been made to address the real and potential risks, with limited improvement. The improvement team in this case consisted of one unit clerk, one regularly scheduled nurse from the rehabilitation department, and one consulting lean coach who facilitated the activities.

The current state map (see Figure CS3.1) was quickly drawn after direct observation of orders being written by a physician and transcribed by the clerk. This activity vividly demonstrated how different perceptions are from the reality of daily work. As the map was drawn and the process boxes with activities within them were reviewed, the difference between a value stream map and a flowchart became very clear. With a conventional flowchart, how the process "should" flow is charted, but with the value stream map, how the work is really happening is made apparent. In addition, and particularly obvious in these observations, were the many activities that do not add value but were "necessary" with the current

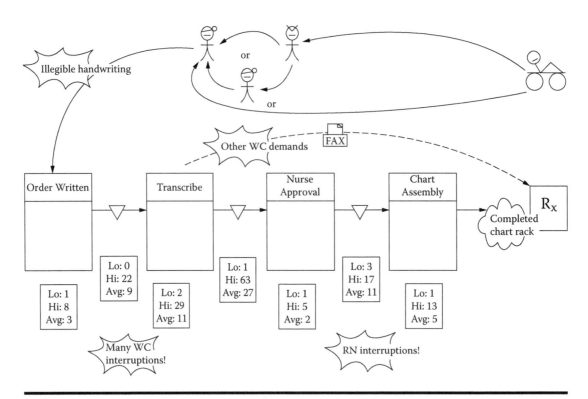

Figure CS3.1

process. In fact, there were so many workarounds exposed in this map that it was decided to list in the deltas the ones that the team agreed occurred routinely.

Although the team could already see obstacles that they could begin working to remove, they decided that for the benefit of changing behaviors and "making a case" for suggested improvements, they would collect data on at least 30 new order transcriptions. They recognized that they could likely collect that information within 2 days and be ready to move forward developing a future state map. This was a smart decision on their part, as demonstrating the waste in measurable time allowed the visual map to speak for itself and made the improvement efforts that they eventually developed indisputable and easy for all to accept.

A very simple data collection tool was designed and printed on fluorescent green paper, which was impossible to miss when attached to the front of the chart. The data points reflected the beginning and end of each of the process steps defined on the current state map. By noon of the second day of collection, the team had acquired information on 30 medication order transcriptions and were ready to evaluate the completed current state map and design a future state map.

Although everyone's first response was to jump to an electronic medication ordering system as the solution, this was recognized as a monument—that is, something that was not currently available to them, but was in the long-term strategic plan of the organization. Recognizing that they were not willing to continue to accept the current state while waiting for the technical option to be available, the team set out to improve what they could with the system they were bound to use. This work contributed nicely to the design of their eventual electronic medical record, and reinforced a rule of process redesign: Do not automate a process until it is understood and can be demonstrated manually!

In this case, the fixes were intended to be immediate, inexpensive, and useful as a test for the eventual electronic upgrade. A list of the current problems was made and each was considered for opportunities. Here is the initial list of problems observed:

- The doctors' handwriting was not always legible, so time was wasted consulting other staff to ensure correct interpretation of the handwriting or multiple phone calls were made to verify the interpretation with the doctor.
- Sometimes orders were written but not appropriately flagged, and the clerk was not aware of the new order on the chart.
- Sometimes there was a delay with the nurse checking the order.
- Sometimes the faxed order to the pharmacy was not received (this led to another observation in the pharmacy revealing that there was no signal when the fax printer ran out of paper).
- Sometimes the nurse would check the order but be called away or forget to enter the new medication on the MAR.
- Sometimes the nurse was called away or forgot to create a new MAR to be included in the MAR notebook.
- Sometimes the MAR notebook was in use and not in its assigned location, and thus was unavailable to the clerk, nurse, or doctor.
- Sometimes a chart with new orders was not returned to the chart rack.

From this list, several problem-solving A3 reports were created to address the specific issues, combining some that were linked to the same root causes. The outcomes of this stopgap approach created an immediate reduction in delays, errors, and potential risk to patient safety with very little investment. Here are a few of the fixes that were quickly implemented:

- A red box was placed in clear sight of the unit clerk and was labeled in large letters: "NEW MEDICATION ORDERS."
- A blue box was placed on the counter and labeled in large letters: "NEW ORDERS TO BE CHECKED BY RN."
- A 24-inch chain was attached to the MAR notebook so that it could not be removed from its assigned location.
- The pharmacy replaced the fax machine with one that sounded an alarm when a transmission could not be printed (due to lack of paper, ink, paper jam, and so on).

Although the human behavior issues such as poor handwriting and memory failure could not be eliminated with this process, communication of the problem in this objective manner and the other visual cues (colored boxes, attached MAR notebook) reminded the staff of the significance of the details that were illuminated in the value stream mapping exercise. This consciousness-raising effort also encouraged the physicians and staff to imagine what they would want in an electronic record and helped contribute thoughtful information to the design of their eventual electronic system.

Case Study 4

Assignment of Transporters for Daytime Inpatient Radiology

This value stream mapping was carried out by a small improvement team led by the manager of the radiology department of a large hospital. Dozens of patients were transported daily from the inpatient units for radiographic services. In spite of accurate knowledge of the length of each procedure and early notification for delivery, maintaining an on-time schedule almost never occurred. Sometimes patients were rescheduled several times for a single procedure and overtime hours were threatening the budget.

Two major problems existed: first, that patients were not arriving on time, and second, congestion of the work area with completed patients waiting for transportation back to the nursing units. As the manager began to look more deeply into the problems, he discovered interesting information about how the transporters were assigned.

Several other common problems were related to late arrivals for procedures, but the manager elected to resolve the transporter assignment issue first. He engaged the manager of transporter services and one transporter, and eventually observed and interviewed a unit clerk and the registered nurse (RN) from the nursing unit who contributed the greatest number of inpatient radiology requests.

This sophisticated hospital with a large campus of three separate buildings used an electronic program for assigning transporters, who picked up a digital pager each day when they arrived for work. When a request was entered into the system for a patient to be delivered to a specific location, the system would notify the transporters in order. The transporter would receive a text message with the time, name, current location, and destination for the patient. Stat response messages were an option for critical clinical situations, and it was noted by the manager that this notification was being abused when a routine patient was delayed.

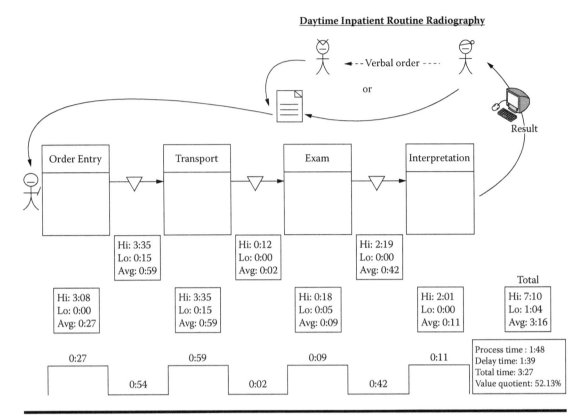

Figure CS4.1

Because the system was electronic, file data were available for the time of the request and transporter dispatch, but it did not record the time that the patient was actually picked up and arrived at his or her destination. Three transporters were chosen to help generate data, and they agreed to note these times and their own location at the time of dispatch.

The current state value stream map that was created (see Figure CS4.1) illustrated occasionally significant delays between dispatch of the busy transporters and arrival at the site of the patient for pickup. After interviewing the transporters and reviewing the data collected by them, it was realized that the system was not being used to recognize the current location of the transporter at the time of dispatch. Because the system dispatched them sequentially, sometimes a dispatcher who had just delivered a patient to radiology would travel to another building for his next assignment while there was a patient in radiology waiting to be returned to his or her room. When the data were added to the map and the value quotient was calculated, only 52% of the transporter's workday was actually spent transporting patients! Almost as much of his time was spent walking across campus to his next assignment.

It was at this point that the managers of radiology and transporter services contacted the vendor of the electronic dispatch system. It was discovered that the system could be reconfigured to dispatch transporters in local zones. With guidance from the vendor, the two managers were able to evaluate transporter usage in the many departments of the hospital and define zones to which transporters could be assigned.

The initial concern was that in some zones the transporters would be very busy, while in others the transporters might be underutilized. The question of adding additional transporters was entertained, but the team was confident that they could rearrange the work without adding staff.

The busy radiology department was used as the test ground, and several trials were run before the zone boundaries were satisfactorily established. No additional staff was required to increase the value quotient on the follow-up map (60 days after the zones were trialed in radiology) to 87%, reflecting a 35% increase in capacity.

Although no initial staff satisfaction survey was conducted before the improvement, radiology and nursing floor staff were queried at 90 days, with 100% responding favorably to the change! While this issue was raised for one diagnostic department, the solution that resulted positively affected every department in the hospital that moves patients.

Case Study 5

Patient Pre-Registration for Day Surgery

This case study is included here to demonstrate the redundancy buried in interdepartmental handoffs and to highlight the significance of this duplicate work to the patient. The work for this value stream map began at the request of the day surgery manager in a busy community hospital. Her initial concern was improving expeditious completion of the following preoperative requirements, which were routinely done the day before the surgical procedure:

- Presurgical lab and radiology testing
- Preoperative (preop) education related to the procedure
- Physical and occupational therapy consultation
- Interview with the pain management team

The work for this lean initiative was done by a university student intern who was working with the author. All pertinent staff were interviewed and observed to validate information, but the focus was from the patient's perspective, and most of the observations were done at the side of one patient traveling through the process. Staff from each department verified that his experience was not unusual and that the value stream map was valid as drawn. The times reflected on the map in Figure CS5.1 reflect only the times experienced by this specific patient.

The procedure was scheduled for the following day. The patient was notified by the surgeon's office to come to the office for a preop history and physical (H&P) with the surgeon's nurse practitioner (NP) after stopping by the lab for routine blood work. In this case, the patient had many surgeries in his history and was taking a number of medications. He arrived at the surgeon's office with two copies of his medical history (including all previous operations) and current medication list. He gave a copy of each to the person who checked him in, to be included in his medical file.

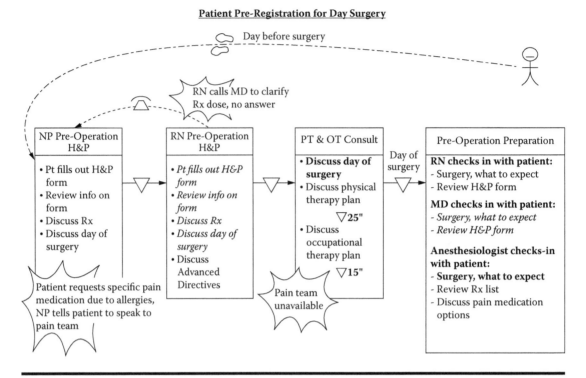

Figure CS5.1

The NP who examined the patient did not have those copies in the room, and the patient gave the NP a second copy during the H&P interview. The only unique information the patient offered during the H&P was his allergy to most pain medications. He stated that for previous surgeries, only one medication was safely and effectively used. The NP voiced that she was uncertain that his preference was in the hospital formulary and recommended that he bring it to the attention of the pain management team in his day surgery pre-admission visit.

The NP then explained in detail what would happen on the day of surgery and about what time to expect to be released. She then directed the patient to proceed to the day surgery area for testing and preop education. (Note that the patient was unaware that the following interviews were planned; he had been told to schedule 1 or 2 hours for the visit to the office. In the end, he spent more than 5 hours at the hospital that day and missed his midday meal.)

When the patient checked in at day surgery, he was shown to the nurse's office, where a registered nurse (RN) from the department asked him the same demographic and history questions that he had just answered in the surgeon's office. These were recorded on the same form used for database input as the one used by the office practice. The RN inquired about previous surgeries and current medications, but the patient could not recall all of the complicated information and dates. The RN called the surgeon's office to clarify dosages that the patient could not remember, but the NP was not available. The RN left a message and awaited a callback.

The nurse also repeated information about what to anticipate for the day of surgery. The only variation from the NP history and physical was signing advanced directives. The RN then walked the patient to another interview room, where the physical therapist (PT) asked him some of the same questions, again went over the activities of the day of surgery, asked about previous surgeries and medications, and developed a plan for postoperative physical therapy. They discussed pain management, and the patient mentioned his allergies and preference for one proven medication. The PT left the room to locate a representative from the pain management team and returned 25 minutes later, without anyone from the team. The PT apologized that no one was available, left again momentarily, and returned with the occupational therapist (OT). The OT asked several of the same questions, repeated what the patient should expect on the day of surgery, concluded her interview, and again went in search of someone from the pain management team. When no one had returned after 15 minutes, the hungry patient left the hospital.

The patient returned for surgery the next morning as directed and was interviewed again by the nurse on duty, the anesthesiologist, and the surgeon. Only then did the anesthesiologist set in motion an effort to find the pain medication requested by the patient.

The outcome? The patient received the correct surgery, but it was delayed in starting by 32 minutes. He recovered and returned home with a supply of the pain medication that was effective for him. But what must this patient think of the caregivers, the doctor's office, and the hospital? Although he was a kindly gentleman, he was observed shaking his head in disbelief and obviously trying to maintain his composure while redundant information was requested and his one true concern was unable to be addressed.

Although the printing of this text precludes the use of color, in reality, this VSM was color coded to indicate when pre-registration activities occurred once, twice, three times, and even in one case, four times. This easy-to-read graphic was extremely effective in demonstrating redundant work and relaying the patient's experience. Reactions to the map launched several structured activities to expedite this process and better prepare clients for stressful surgical events.

Case Study 6

Trauma Patient Flow in a Busy Emergency Room

This high-level lean initiative was done in a very busy, inner-city, Level II trauma center. The acuity of patients was very high, and care was urgent, as they saw many patients with major penetrating and blunt traumas.

The emergency department (ED) staff and trauma surgeons who cared for these patients felt that sometimes it took too long to complete assessments, diagnostics, treatments, and disposition decisions. The average length of stay in the ED for each patient was more than 4 hours. The staff and trauma surgeons believed there were opportunities to reduce the amount of time in the department without sacrificing the quality of care.

The original trauma patient throughput improvement team consisted of the following:

- ED medical director
- ED nursing director
- ED clinical nurse specialist
- ED staff registered nurses (RNs; one day shift, one evening shift, one night shift)
- ED patient care technician
- Chief of trauma
- ED unit clerk

As A3 go-forwards were identified, the following members were added to specific A3 teams:

- Operating room (OR) nursing director
- Intensive care unit (ICU) nursing director
- Director of hospital admissions

■ Director of radiology/imaging
■ Director of the laboratory
■ Radiology technician
■ Respiratory therapist
■ Representative from central stores
■ Representative from environmental services
■ ED registrar
■ ED staff physicians
■ Director of the blood bank
■ Representative from the bed control office

The current state value stream map was drawn as shown in Figure CS6.1.

A limited amount of data was electronically available on the trauma patient's throughput in the ED:

■ Time of arrival in the ED
■ Mode of arrival
■ Time first seen by an ED doctor
■ Time first seen by a trauma surgeon
■ Time of transfer
■ Patient disposition

The team realized that they needed additional data in order to determine if activities in each process box were appropriate or not and if there were opportunities for waste reduction. In order to do this, 10 additional trauma cases on various shifts were observed by the ED clinical nurse specialist, the ED nursing director, and the ED staff RNs to collect and validate the areas that existing file data did not provide. Spaghetti maps were drawn and copious notes were taken to record activities (or lack of activities) before, during, and after major trauma patient resuscitations in the ED.

All information collected during the observations was reviewed by the trauma patient throughput improvement team. From the review of the information compiled on the current state map the team began to construct a future state map that they collectively agreed would improve care and reduce waste of staff resources.

It was decided that there was one opportunity to combine process boxes: in the area where the patient was returned to the ED from diagnostic imaging. The team decided that at the point of diagnostic imaging, a disposition decision should be made and the patient transferred to the appropriate department directly from imaging without returning to the ED. This change was added to the future state map. In addition, 15 specific problem areas were identified on the current state map that were recognized as roadblocks that kept caregivers from delivering the model they designed on the future state map. Each of these specific issues was addressed using A3 problem solving:

Major Trauma Patient Flow Through ED

Figure CS6.1

- Too many people (and noise and confusion) in the trauma room
- Nonspecific role definition for some trauma response team members
- Lost learning opportunities for students (interns, residents, nursing, EMS, and so on)
- Too much movement in and around the trauma room
- Missing supplies in the trauma room
- No warm blankets in the trauma room
- Inconsistent use of universal precaution garb by some trauma team members
- Difficulty ordering diagnostic tests when patient was a John or Jane Doe
- Delay in obtaining O-negative blood (especially on evenings, nights, weekends)
- Poor documentation
- Difficult for radiology technician to take timely X-rays in trauma room
- Poor communication with OR, lab, and blood bank
- Delay in making a disposition when the patient was in imaging, necessitating a return trip to the ED
- Difficulty restocking the trauma room in preparation for the next patient
- Missed charges for stock used

The improvement team discovered that many of the problems that caused delays with trauma patient throughput in the ED were multidisciplinary issues that had to be addressed by representatives from each involved department in order to eliminate them. When the maps were used to demonstrate the big picture of the flow and the problems (both current and future) it was easy to engage other departments quickly, as they could visually recognize their role in the overall activity.

The significance of the implementation plan was that any department that was a "player" in an issue was brought to the table to be part of that specific improvement team. By inviting members of the other departments in addition to the ED to the team, problems were solved in a multidisciplinary way, and there was ownership of the problem resolution. In addition, ideas were presented that may not have occurred to the ED improvement team. A willingness to make changes in their own work was present that would have been less likely if they had not been part of creating a better way to work.

For example, regarding the difficulty obtaining O-negative blood, the blood bank offered to place a small refrigerator in the ED, keep four units of O-negative blood in it, check it every day, keep it locked, and rotate blood that was close to expiring into the hospital's main blood supply, replacing the ED blood with newer units. The ED team would likely not have thought of this solution, and if they did, the blood bank personnel may have balked at the suggestion. Because the blood bank representative brought the idea to the table, it was well received by lab staff and they were willing to tweak the process in trials. This was ultimately an integral part of getting blood on demand to critical trauma victims.

Regarding missing supplies, difficulty restocking the trauma room in a timely manner, and capturing charges, the central stores representative offered to stock and provide trauma supply exchange carts for the ED. Three carts were kept in the ED (one in each trauma room and an extra one in the ED supply room) and two additional carts were maintained and ready in central stores. A large bin on the bottom shelf of each cart was used for instruments. When the patient left the ED, the cart was closed and labeled with the patient's name. Central stores personnel retrieved the cart from the ED on request, brought a replacement cart, and, when restocking the cart, completed a "used supplies" slip that generated accurate charges for each specific patient. Similar to the O-negative blood problem resolved by the blood bank, central stores offered unique and workable solutions for this long-standing and previously expensive issue.

As follow-up, A3 plans were prioritized and implementation plans were tested and revised over a 6-month period. After each A3 plan was implemented, observations were made by various members of the team to determine whether the plan was effective. Each implementation plan and outcome data were reviewed monthly at the trauma committee meeting. Using visual documents to report the improvements was quick and effective—even to committee members who were not familiar with lean documents and language.

Overall throughput follow-up data was collected at 1, 3, and 6 months after implementation. At 6 months, when all identified A3 implementation plans had been completed, 10 major trauma patient observations took place. The average throughput time for each of these patients was less than 2 hours, a reduction in throughput time of 50%. The team not only met, but exceeded, its original goal of admitting major trauma patients within 3 hours.

As the team and all ED staff first saw small, and then larger, changes occur, the enthusiasm for problem solving increased. After 6 months, when the results were reported (as well as acknowledged and celebrated!), they were eager to take on even more improvements.

The following is a short list of their follow-up plan:

■ Review the original future state map and conduct a new current state map to identify even more opportunities for improvement.
■ Continue monitoring and improving A3 implementation plans.
■ Identify new issues to address with A3 plans.
■ Compare morbidity and mortality data from the time preceding the throughput project and every 6 months after the start of the project to evaluate the overall effect of the shortened length of stay on trauma patient outcomes.

Total Joint Replacement Scheduling (Operating Room Back-Table Set-Up)

The total joint replacement scheduling process was selected for improvement by the orthopedic service line coordinator in order to standardize the back-table instrument setup and improve the operating room (OR) turnaround time. There was no standard format for spreading the instruments, which made it difficult for the team to work effectively, particularly when covering breaks and interchanging staff. It was routine for cases not to start on time. The improvement team consisted of the OR director, the orthopedic service line coordinator, a surgery technician, a registered nurse (RN) from the orthopedic patient care floor, and an OR nurse who regularly worked the orthopedic rooms.

To create the first value stream map, the OR schedulers were interviewed individually. They were asked to simulate scheduling a total joint replacement (TJR) procedure and talk the improvement team through a typical day. From these interviews and simulations, a current state map (see Figure CS7.1) was drawn by the team and validated for accuracy by the schedulers. Problems with the flow of work began to emerge as soon as the steps were put on paper.

From the map, a simple data collection tool was devised and the schedulers agreed to collect the times for each step on the following Monday and Tuesday, when 11 appropriate cases were scheduled. The team agreed that they would continue to collect data for 3 weeks to ensure statistical significance, but they were confident that after 1 week the numbers would support their experience-based assumptions. At the end of the first week they were all surprised to notice roadblocks that they had not anticipated, but that were contributing significantly to their OR start delays and the frustration of physicians, OR staff, and schedulers. Imagine the concern of families in the waiting room!

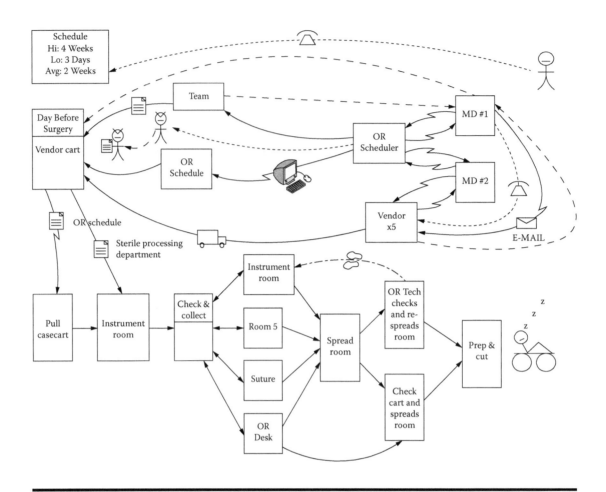

Figure CS7.1

Once the team created the current state map, they realized that the problem they initially identified, back-table instrument spread, was being caused by upstream problems with the case information on the OR schedule that originated in the surgeons' offices. Five different scheduling forms were being used by the orthopedic practices and recopied by medical assistants, then carried through a chain of three people before arrival at the OR secretary's desk. The information needed by staff regarding the joint replacement system being used was either incomplete or inaccurate 100% of the time! Needless to say, the staff had been aware that the work was problematic, but was astounded to see the data that confirmed the level of failure.

The likelihood of not having the needed equipment was related to a number of seemingly small factors. No one prepared instruments for a case until the morning of surgery, so start times were delayed up to 20 minutes in almost every case while waiting for the surgeon or vendor to provide the necessary information for the staff to pull the correct equipment. To compensate for the poor process, OR staff members were sometimes coming to work 30 minutes early to work around the problem, resulting in an increase in overtime payroll hours. One scrub technician started going to the surgeon's office the night before each case to get the needed information so that she could get her work done on time the next day. Frustration experienced by the staff and physicians was very high and frequently resulted in an unpleasant work atmosphere.

As an implementation plan, the team developed a form based on the information they needed to get the surgical room ready for an on-time start. They oriented the medical assistants and surgeons to the new form, it was approved, and it was being used by all five orthopedic offices within 1 week.

A similar initiative had been tried 6 months earlier and failed because these same staff members did not see the whole picture of the flow of necessary activities required to prepare for on-time surgery, nor could they appreciate the scale and detail of the problems created. The office staff resisted the previous change and wanted to stay with their own familiar forms. The service line coordinator acknowledged that even from her position she did not see the whole picture prior to the value stream mapping (VSM) and had been attempting to standardize a form without an understanding of upstream and downstream effects.

With the team's newly developed confidence and competence in problem solving, they decided to tackle the long-standing, nationwide, elusive problem of sterile wraps. The map pointed out how much rework and delay was being caused by resterilizing (also known as "flashing") instruments due to puncture holes in the sterile wrapping material. This problem not only caused rework and waste for staff and delays in OR start times, but also posed a risk of infection to patients if a hole in the sterile wrap went undetected.

The staff was working around the problem with a time-consuming, awkward, and risky step of visually scanning each wrap for holes. One technician would hold the tray (weighing approximately 60 pounds) while another held the large blue wrapper up to a light to search for holes. The team collected paper wraps for 1 week and detected holes in 50% of them! OR cases were delayed an average of 22 minutes each time holes were found and the tray had to be flashed.

After considering all options, the team decided to purchase reusable sterile containers at a total cost of $53,000 for the orthopedic joint replacement program. They tried to avoid this expense, but it quickly became obvious that the cost would be recovered in a short time. The cost of the disposable paper wraps was weighed against this purchase figure and it was determined that the reusable containers would be paid for in 46 months, given current usage. The wasted OR time at $58 per minute was not factored in, nor was doctor time. The potential for adding cases and increasing capacity was discussed and projected. The team used an A3 report to illustrate the details of the problem and the proposed remediation and made their case with administration. It was approved immediately as an exception to the existing budget.

The team also made some interesting discoveries:

■ Working with the current state map allowed the team to "see" the flow of the process from the initial request to the preparation of the patient in the OR. The graphic depiction illustrated loops in the information flow and led to the discovery that problems with spreading the back-table were caused by a lack of information from the physicians' offices. The process of mapping and understanding the entire process made prioritizing the improvements evident. Without this insight, the team may have wasted time addressing a process failure rather than ferreting out the root cause.

■ The initial intent was to focus on the opinion of one individual to improve turnover time. Through the process of mapping and seeing the whole process, as well as validating and evaluating it with all the affected parties, a systematic approach to repairing the process was obvious, was objective, and left no key players out of the improvement.

■ The team members blossomed in this work environment, where they had previously felt stifled and powerless to make improvements. Problem solving is now a part of their daily routine.

■ The lean approach led to rapid alignment of efforts and agreement among individuals and groups that had previously not worked in concert.

With the two major issues addressed, additional planned improvements derived from this mapping work but not yet completed at the time of this writing include the following:

■ Coordination and consolidation of surgeon preferences for back-table spread of instruments. The value stream map led the team (and the surgeons) to recognize the complexity of each surgeon preferring a slightly different setup.

■ Standardizing case carts to match the new streamlined preferences that resulted from the new forms used in the department.

■ Standardizing the spread of instruments done by night-shift technicians and daytime technicians according to joint room standards, which are based on safety issues. It is anticipated that this step alone will reduce 10 to 20 minutes of rework by the daytime technician for each case.

■ The paper sterile wrap issue has expanded to the infectious disease department. After piloting the new sterile containers in the orthopedic joint replacement program they will be evaluated for application to the entire OR and other treatment areas of the organization. Despite considerable up-front expense, the cost:benefit ratio was measurable, and decisions about where to make this change can be made with pragmatic evaluation based on data and experience.

This experience was the first for this OR team as they were learning the lean framework, VSM, and A3 tools. A key success factor in their ability to solve these problems quickly was the engagement of the OR director and administration.

The team is now meeting for 2 hours every 2 weeks to continue problem solving and to sustain and further improve their initial work.

The graphic representation of the work and problems on the value stream map and A3 reports led to rapid understanding and cooperation of the surgeons. Their ability to see the whole story was a critical part of this process.

Index

ABOUT THE AUTHOR

Cindy Jimmerson is a pioneer of lean health-care, having initiated her work with a grant from the National Science Foundation (2001–2004). She is the founder and president of Lean Healthcare West, an organization of healthcare professionals offering education and implementation of TPS/lean principles in hospital, clinic, and long-term care facilities. She is the author of the reVIEW© Course and Workbook and many journal publications. Although she travels internationally for work, she refuses to budge her office from the beautiful Blackfoot River in Missoula, Montana.

Lightning Source UK Ltd.
Milton Keynes UK
UKHW052036160519
342835UK00010B/91/P

9 781420 078527